AS Psychology
UNIT 3
2ND EDITION

AQA

Specification A

Module 3: Social Psych
and Research Meth

Alison Wadeley & Mike Cardwell

Philip Allan Updates
Market Place
Deddington
Oxfordshire
OX15 0SE

tel: 01869 338652
fax: 01869 337590
e-mail: sales@philipallan.co.uk
www.philipallan.co.uk

© Philip Allan Updates 2001
This edition © Philip Allan Updates 2002

ISBN 0 86003 892 0

This Guide has been written specifically to support students preparing for the AQA Specification A AS Psychology Unit 3 examination. The content has been neither approved nor endorsed by AQA and remains the sole responsibility of the authors.

Printed by Raithby, Lawrence & Co Ltd, Leicester

Contents

Introduction

About this guide 4

The examination: AO1, AO2 and AO3 questions 5

How are the marks awarded for Social Psychology questions? 7

How are the marks awarded for Research Methods questions? 8

■ ■ ■

Content Guidance

About this section 10

Social psychology

Conformity and minority influence 11

Obedience to authority 14

Critical issue: ethical issues in psychological research 18

Social psychology: defining the terms 21

Research methods

Quantitative and qualitative research methods 23

Research design and implementation 27

Data analysis 32

Research methods: defining the terms 37

■ ■ ■

Questions and Answers

About this section 40

Q1 Social psychology (I) 41

Q2 Social psychology (II) 45

Q3 Social psychology (III) 49

Q4 Social psychology (IV) 53

Q5 Research methods (I) 57

Q6 Research methods (II) 62

Introduction

About this guide

This is a guide to Unit 3 of AQA(A) AS Psychology, which examines the content of **Module 3: Social Psychology and Research Methods**. This guide is intended as a revision *aid*, rather than a textbook or revision guide. Therefore, the emphasis is on *how* the specification content is examined and on showing you how different levels of answer to sample questions will be assessed.

The two compulsory sections of Social Psychology and Research Methods are covered, and for each of these we take you through the following:
- the specification content for each topic. This is fully explained so that you know exactly what you might be asked to demonstrate in an examination.
- appropriate content relevant to those topics. This gives you a minimal coverage of each topic area. This is not intended as the *only* appropriate content for a given topic area, but does give you an idea of how you might present your answer to a question set on this particular aspect of the specification.
- a set of definitions of key terms for each section, vital for those 'What is meant by?' questions. Each of these has been constructed to be succinct but informative and therefore appropriate for such questions.
- *four* sample questions for Social Psychology and *two* for Research Methods. Each is accompanied by full explanations of its requirements. These questions demonstrate the typical format of AQA(A) AS questions, as well as the appropriate breakdown of marks between AO1 and AO2 skills (see below).
- a typical 'grade B or C' student response to each of these questions, together with examiner comments showing where the marks have been gained and lost.
- a 'grade A' response to each of these questions, showing how they might have been answered by a very good student.

How to use this guide

This book is not intended as a set of model answers to examination questions, nor as an account of the *right* material to include should you be asked to display this very same knowledge. It is intended to give you an idea of the way that your examination will be structured and how you might improve your own examination performance.

It is suggested that you read through the relevant section in Content Guidance before attempting a question from the Question and Answer section, and only read the specimen answers after you have tackled the question yourself.

The examination:
AO1, AO2 and AO3 questions

Unit 3 is assessed in a 1 hour examination or as part of a 3 hour AS examination that covers all three units. Your examination paper will comprise *three* questions, two of which are on Social Psychology and one on Research Methods. You are required to select *one* on Social Psychology and answer all parts of the Research Methods question.

Each question is worth *30 marks*. Within each Social Psychology question, there will be *three* parts. The last part of each question is always the **AO1** + **AO2** part of the question, and the two preceding parts are **AO1**. The **AO1** question parts (and the **AO1** part of the **AO1** + **AO2** question) test your *knowledge and understanding* skills, while the **AO2** component of the final part of each question tests your skills of *analysis and evaluation*. In each question, the **AO1** component is worth *18 marks* and the **AO2** component *12 marks*. In the final part of each question there are 6 marks for **AO1** and 12 for **AO2**.

The Research Methods question (also worth 30 marks) will present you with a hypothetical piece of research and ask you a number of questions (usually between 7 and 11 in total) that assess your **AO1** skills (3 marks), your **AO2** skills (6 marks) and your **AO3** skills (21 marks). The **AO3** assessment applies only to Research Methods questions, and is an assessment of your ability to 'design and comment on psychological investigation(s), choosing from a range of methods, and taking into account the issues of reliability, validity and ethics, draw conclusions from data'.

Questions

The following are *examples* of the types of Social Psychology question that are used to assess AO1 and AO2.

AO1 questions
What is meant by the terms 'obedience', 'ecological validity' and 'informed consent'?
(2+2+2 marks)

Describe two differences between majority (conformity) and minority influence.
(3+3 marks)

Describe the aims/procedures/findings/conclusions* of one study of obedience to authority.
(6 marks)
[*any combination of two of these aspects of the study]

Outline two explanations of why people yield to minority influence.
(3+3 marks)

Outline research into conformity.
(6 marks)

Give two criticisms of the research study outlined in... *(3+3 marks)*

AO1 + AO2 questions
With reference to one or more research studies of social influence, *consider* whether such research might be criticised as unethical. *(18 marks)*

To what extent have psychologists been successful in dealing with the ethical issues that arise in psychological research? *(18 marks)*

'Laboratory studies of obedience are rarely convincing, either in the deception of participants or in their ability to explain obedience in the real world.'
To what extent are such criticisms of the validity of obedience research justified?
(18 marks)

Effective exam performance

- *Read the questions carefully*, as marks are only available for the specific require-ments of the question set. Miss those out and you lose marks; include something irrelevant and you have wasted valuable time.

- Remember that *each mark* is equivalent to approximately *1 minute* of thinking and writing, so it is vital to use this time wisely, neither extending it nor skimping on it.

- *Make a brief plan* before answering the question. This can be in your head or on paper, but you must know where you are going and how long it will take you to get there. *Time management is absolutely vital.*

- Sometimes questions ask you to *outline* something. You need to practise doing this as the skill of précis is not as easy as it looks.

- *Be aware of the difference between AO1, AO2 and AO3 questions.* AO1 + AO2 questions are not just an opportunity for more descriptive content. You must *engage with the question topic* in the required way.

- In AO1 questions, the emphasis is on the *amount* of relevant material presented (e.g. 'limited' or 'basic'), the amount of *detail* given (e.g. 'lacking detail') and the *accuracy* of the material (e.g. 'muddled').

- For the AO2 component of AO1 + AO2 question parts, the emphasis is on the *amount* and *level* of the critical commentary (e.g. 'superficial'), its *thoroughness* (e.g. 'reasonably thorough') and how *effectively* it has been used (e.g. 'highly effective').

- Questions that assess AO3 skills require you to put your research methods skills to work in order to solve a particular psychological problem.

How are the marks awarded for Social Psychology questions?

Mark allocations for AO1 2-mark questions

What is meant by the terms 'obedience', 'ecological validity' and 'informed consent'?
(2+2+2 marks)

Marks	Criteria
2 marks	Accurate and detailed
1 mark	Basic, lacking detail, muddled or flawed
0 marks	Inappropriate or incorrect

Mark allocations for AO1 3- and 6-mark questions

Outline two explanations of why people yield to minority influence. *(3+3 marks)*

Outline research into conformity. *(6 marks)*

3-mark questions	6-mark questions	Criteria
3 marks	6–5 marks	Accurate and detailed
2 marks	4–3 marks	Limited, generally accurate but less detailed
1 mark	2–1 marks	Basic, lacking in detail, muddled or flawed
0 marks	0 marks	Inaccurate or irrelevant

Mark allocations for AO2

Certain questions are AO1 + AO2. They are awarded 18 marks: 6 marks AO1 (assessed using the criteria above) and 12 marks AO2, assessed according to the criteria below. The heading '**commentary**' applies to the specific AO2 requirement of the question (e.g. 'evaluate' or 'to what extent?').

Marks	Commentary	Analysis	Use of material
12–11	Informed	Reasonably thorough	Effective
10–9	Reasonable	Slightly limited	Effective
8–7	Reasonable	Limited	Reasonably effective
6–5	Basic	Limited	Reasonably effective
4–3	Superficial	Rudimentary	Minimal interpretation
2–1	Just discernible	Weak and muddled	Mainly irrelevant
0	Wholly irrelevant	Wholly irrelevant	Wholly irrelevant

How are the marks awarded for Research Methods questions?

Mark allocations for 2-mark questions

State a suitable directional hypothesis for this study.   *(2 marks)*

Marks	Criteria
2 marks	Accurate and informed
1 mark	Brief or muddled
0 marks	Inappropriate or incorrect

Mark allocations for 1-mark questions

What type of experimental design was used in this investigation?   *(1 mark)*

Marks	Criteria
1 mark	Accurate
0 marks	Inappropriate or incorrect

Content
Guidance

In this section, content guidance is offered on the topics of social influence (Social Psychology) and Research Methods in psychology.

Each topic begins with an outline and explanation of the AQA Specification A requirement for this part of the module. This is followed by a more detailed look at the theories and studies that make up the module content for Social Psychology and the methodological issues and practices that make up the Research Methods section.

Knowledge of appropriate theories and studies is essential for the AS examination. It is also important to be able to assess the value of these theories and studies, and this is done in regular 'Evaluation' features.

At the end of each topic, definitions are provided for key terms — some of which you might be asked to define in an examination.

Names and publication dates have been given when referring to research studies. The full references for these studies should be available in textbooks should the reader wish to research the topic further.

Social psychology

Conformity and minority influence

Specification content

Research studies into conformity (e.g. Sherif, Asch, Zimbardo) and minority influence (e.g. Moscovici, Clark). Explanations of why people yield to majority (conformity) and minority influence.

Here you are expected to know about **conformity** and **minority influence** as forms of social influence. You are specifically required to know *explanations* for why people yield to these two forms of social influence. As the specification uses 'explanations' in the plural, you should know at least two explanations for conformity and two for minority influence. Note that **conformity** and **majority influence** are the same thing, whereas **minority influence** is something completely different.

The use of the term 'research studies' should alert you to the probability of questions relating to *studies* in these two areas. The examples given (e.g. Asch, Zimbardo, Moscovici) are simply examples of appropriate studies and cannot be prescribed in a question. These are, however, good ones to revise. When revising research studies in these areas, make sure you can summarise the *aims, procedures, findings* and *conclusions* of each one.

Conformity

Conformity is a form of social influence that results from exposure to the opinions of a majority. It is the tendency for people to adopt the behaviour, attitudes and values of other members of a reference group.

Research evidence

Asch (1956)

The aim of Asch's original study was to explore the conditions under which participants would remain independent when faced with a fairly unambiguous perceptual task and a majority opinion that differed from their own judgement of the task.

Asch showed a series of lines to participants seated around a table. All but one of the participants were confederates of the researcher. In each trial, participants were shown a 'test' line, and asked which of three other lines was the same length. In six neutral trials, the confederates gave correct answers; in the other 12 they unanimously gave the same incorrect answer.

In 32% of the trials where confederates had unanimously given a wrong answer, naïve participants conformed to the majority view; 74% of the naïve participants conformed at least once (compared with only 5% when making decisions in private).

Asch's study found that some people conformed to the majority because they believed that their perception must have been inaccurate and the majority's accurate. Others yielded because they didn't want to risk being ridiculed by the rest of the group. Asch found that despite the pressure exerted by the majority, a large proportion of people tended to remain independent in their judgements.

Evaluation

- Perrin and Spencer (1981) claim that the Asch studies reflect a particular historical and cultural perspective (the American era of McCarthyism) where conformity was highly valued. They suggest that such conformity effects are no longer evident in similar experimental studies unless the majority are perceived by the naïve participant as having greater social status.
- Smith and Bond (1998), in a review of 31 studies of conformity, suggest that conformity to a majority is more likely in collectivist cultures than in individualist cultures (like the UK and US). Thus, conformity can be seen as a positive feature in cultures where interdependence is more highly valued than independence.

Zimbardo et al. (1973)

Zimbardo et al. used a prison simulation to investigate the extent to which people would conform to social roles when they were exposed to a strange and anonymous situation. The study also aimed to investigate the degree to which 'victims' are dehumanised by those who are given legitimate power to control them.

They used 24 male volunteers, judged to be both physically and mentally healthy, allocated randomly to the roles of prisoners or guards. The prisoners were 'arrested' at their homes and, after being initially processed by the police, handed over to the guards.

Although Zimbardo et al. intended the study to last 2 weeks, they had to stop it after 6 days. The guards continually harassed and humiliated the prisoners. Some guards behaved in a brutal and sadistic manner. The prisoners initially revolted, but became increasingly passive and docile. Some prisoners had to be released from the study before its conclusion because they showed symptoms of severe emotional disturbance.

Zimbardo et al.'s study showed the power of social roles and the tendency for aggressive behaviour to be heightened when carried out during the enactment of legitimate social roles and when both the perpetrator of the aggression and the victim are both de-personalised (the process of **deindividuation**).

Evaluation

- Savin (1973) believed that 'the ends did not justify the means' in this study. Although it is claimed that the study was influential in radically altering the way that American prisons are run, in truth, the American prison system has become more impersonal, rather than less impersonal, in the days since Zimbardo et al.'s study.
+ Zimbardo et al. claimed that studies such as this and the study carried out by Milgram are criticised because they 'open our eyes' to the possibilities that all of us are capable of conformity to destructive social roles.

Minority influence

This is a form of social influence whereby people reject the established norm of the majority of group members and move to the position of the minority.

Research evidence

Moscovici et al. (1969)

Research has generally found that, in order for a minority to have an influence over a majority, a number of conditions are necessary. Moscovici et al. were interested in whether **consistent** expression of a position was an important factor in explaining the process of minority influence.

Participants were required to describe the colour of 36 slides. Of the six participants, two were confederates of the experimenter. The slides used were all blue, but the use of different filters varied their brightness. In the **consistent** condition of the experiment, the two confederates called all 36 slides green. In the **inconsistent** condition, the two confederates called 24 of the slides green and the remaining 12 slides blue.

Participants in the consistent condition yielded in 8.42% of all trials. Participants in the inconsistent condition yielded in only 1.25% of the trials. In an extension to this study, both experimental groups showed a lower threshold for green than a control group, i.e. they were more likely to report ambiguous blue/green stimuli as green.

Moscovici et al.'s study demonstrated that a minority *can* be influential in changing the opinions of a majority, but only if they remain consistent in their position throughout. This study also demonstrated that this form of influence can produce more long-lasting changes, indicating that such influence does not merely lead to public compliance.

Evaluation

− Research has generally found that participants tend to converge on the views of the majority. Exposure to minority influence, however, stimulates more active and detailed information processing which might increase the probability of correct answers.

+ Although exposure to a minority position might not change public acceptance of that position, it can increase the likelihood of a private change in attitudes. Maas and Clark (1983) studied the effects of exposure to majority and minority opinions on gay rights. Although participants conformed publicly to the views of the majority, exposure to the views of a minority produced a change in privately expressed attitudes.

Clark (1994)

The aim of this study was to investigate how minority influence might work in simulated jury settings, thus providing a real-life application of the processes of minority influence.

Student jurors read a summary of the film *Twelve Angry Men* in which one juror gradually changes the minds of the other members of the jury concerning the innocence of a man accused of murder. In the first condition of this study, students read the whole script of *Twelve Angry Men*. In the second condition, students were made aware of the fact that the main character was unconvinced of the man's guilt but were not aware of his arguments to support this position. In the third condition, students knew of the dissenting juror's arguments but did not receive information about other jury members changing their opinions.

Knowing both the arguments *and* the behaviour of other group members affected the student jurors' decision regarding the man's guilt. Reading the arguments was sufficient to persuade many of the student jurors, but knowledge that others had also changed their minds increased this effect.

This study demonstrated that consistent and unwavering presentation of a minority position can encourage people to question their own position on an issue. This effect is enhanced if others are known also to have changed their minds, thus reducing the discomfort that accompanies social conflict and disagreement with others.

Explanations for why people yield to majority influence (conformity)

Normative social influence is an explanation for conformity as a consequence of people's desire not to infringe group norms. This often occurs because people want to be seen as part of a group rather than deviant from it.

Informational social influence occurs when we turn to others in an attempt to gain information about how to think or act. This type of conformity is common when people are uncertain about their own opinions or how to behave in a specific situation, and therefore must rely on others for guidance.

Explanations for why people yield to minority influence

If a minority opinion continues to be expressed despite the inhibitory pressure of majority disagreement, its impact is increased. This causes the majority to take the minority view seriously. If some members of the majority 'defect' to this position, it can set up a 'snowball' effect, whereby minority influence becomes more pronounced.

The dissociation model (Perez et al., 1995) argues that minority influence occurs because, over time, there is a **disassociation** between an idea and its source. Initially ideas are resisted *because* they arise from a deviant minority, yet gradually they become detached from this source and are remembered without the inhibitory 'ownership' of the minority.

Obedience to authority

Specification content

Research studies into obedience to authority (e.g. Milgram, Hofling, Meuus, Raaijmakers). Issues of experimental and ecological validity associated with such research. Explanations of psychological processes involved in obedience, the reasons why people obey and how people might resist obedience.

Here you are expected to know about **obedience to authority** as a form of social influence. As in the previous subsection, the term 'research studies' is used and examples are given to guide you. It is necessary to study at least *two studies* of obedience. You might choose the work of two different researchers (or teams of researchers), such as Milgram and Hofling, or you might choose two studies carried out by the same researcher (Milgram explored many different aspects of the relationship between authority and obedience).

You are also required to know about **experimental** and **ecological validity** in the context of obedience research. It is worth finding out what critics of Milgram's research said about validity issues, and how Milgram responded to such claims. You are specifically required to know *explanations* for the processes involved in obedience (i.e. what *causes* people to obey and how they might *resist* obedience). As the specification uses 'explanations' in the plural, you should know at least two explanations for obedience and, likewise, more than one reason why people obey.

Obedience to authority

This is a type of social influence whereby somebody acts in response to a direct order from another person. There is also the implication that the person receiving the order is made to respond in a way that they would not otherwise have done without the order.

Research evidence
Milgram (1963)
One of the main aims of Milgram's research into obedience to authority was to explore the circumstances under which people might be induced to act against their conscience by inflicting harm on other people. This was born out of the need to explain the behaviour of those who committed atrocities in Second World War death camps.

Milgram deceived 40 male volunteer participants into thinking they that were giving gradually increasing electric shocks to another participant (an actor) during a word association task. The 'real' subject acted as the 'teacher' and the actor was the 'learner'. In the 'baseline' condition, the learner was in another room, with no voice contact with the teacher. After each wrong answer an electric shock was delivered (although none was really given) with an increase of 15 volts each time, rising to 450 volts.

All 40 participants continued to at least the 300-volt level; 65% continued to the full 450 volts. Milgram found that the closer the 'teacher' was to the 'learner', the more likely they were to refuse the experimenter's command to deliver the shocks. He also discovered that obedience levels were lower when the experimenter was not physically present and gave orders over the telephone.

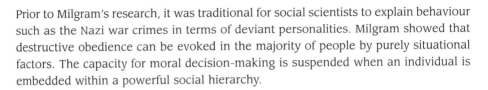

Prior to Milgram's research, it was traditional for social scientists to explain behaviour such as the Nazi war crimes in terms of deviant personalities. Milgram showed that destructive obedience can be evoked in the majority of people by purely situational factors. The capacity for moral decision-making is suspended when an individual is embedded within a powerful social hierarchy.

Evaluation

- Baumrind (1964) criticised Milgram's research on the grounds that it was not ethically justified. She claimed that participants suffered considerable distress which was not justified given the aims of the research. However, in a follow-up survey, 84% of Milgram's participants indicated that they were 'glad to have taken part', and felt they had learned something extremely valuable about themselves.
- Baumrind also claimed that participants would suffer permanent psychological harm from their participation in the study, including a loss of self-esteem and distrust of authority. However, psychiatric examinations 1 year later showed no sign of psychological damage attributable to participation in the research.

Hofling (1966)

The aim of this study was to see whether obedience to an authority figure (in this case a doctor) would be evident in a real-life setting, where participants were not aware that they were taking part in a psychological study.

Hofling et al. arranged for nurses in a hospital ward to receive a telephone call from an unknown doctor. Each unsuspecting nurse was asked to administer a drug (Astroten) to a patient before the doctor arrived. To have done so meant breaking a number of hospital rules, including giving twice the maximum dose for the drug, accepting a telephone instruction from an unknown doctor, and acting without written instructions.

Despite this, 21 out of 22 nurses agreed to administer the drug (which was actually a harmless placebo), thus lending some support to Milgram's claim that obedience would also be evident in natural settings.

This study demonstrated that obedience to authority *does* occur in real-life settings — in this case a significant majority of nurses were willing to break hospital regulations if told to do so by a higher-status figure. One must be cautious about accepting this as a real-life situation, however, as several aspects of the study were unnecessarily contrived (fictional drug, unknown doctor, etc.).

Evaluation

- Rank and Jacobson (1977) criticised the Hofling et al. study because the nurses had no knowledge of the drug involved (Astroten). In a replication of the study, the common drug Valium was used. This had the effect of lowering the likelihood that nurses would exceed the maximum dosage for this drug.
- Rank and Jacobson also pointed out that the nurses in Hofling et al.'s study had

no opportunity to seek advice before administering the drug (a common practice on hospital wards). In the replication, nurses were able to speak to other nurses before proceeding. This, together with the use of Valium rather than Astroten, meant that only two out of 18 nurses administered the drug as requested by the absent doctor.

Experimental and ecological validity of obedience research

Experimental validity

Orne and Holland (1968) claimed that Milgram's research lacked experimental validity, i.e. participants had not been deceived at all, and therefore the conclusions drawn from the study were inappropriate. According to this claim, participants had not *believed* that they were giving electric shocks, and pretended to be distressed as part of their 'role' in the experiment. Milgram defended his original claim through evidence from debriefing sessions (participants admitted they had believed they were giving shocks) and through film evidence where participants appeared in considerable distress when delivering the shocks.

Ecological validity

Orne and Holland's second claim was that the study lacked ecological validity, having been carried out in the psychology lab of a prestigious American university (Yale). However, when Milgram carried out a replication in some run-down office buildings, he found that obedience levels, although lower (around 48%), were still far higher than predicted at the beginning of the research. This finding does, however, demonstrate that changing the legitimacy of the authority figure (greater in Yale) does make a difference to obedience.

Psychological processes involved in obedience research

Once subjects are actually part of the experiment, **binding factors** begin to operate. Various cues (the experimenter's status and manner, the volunteer status of the subject) increase the pressure on the participant to continue. As participants have already given lower-level shocks, it becomes hard to resist the experimenter's requirement to increase the shocks as the experiment continues.

The subject is able to shift the responsibility for their actions onto another person (in this case the experimenter) through the process of **agentic shift**. They now see themselves as the **agents** of another person (the authority figure) and no longer responsible for their own actions.

In Milgram's original study, the teacher and learner were in different rooms, with the teacher protected (i.e. **buffered**) from having to see their 'victim', and also from the consequences of the electric shocks. When the learner was in the same room, this buffering effect was reduced, as was the tendency to obey the commands of the experimenter, and therefore the overall level of obedience.

Why do people obey?

Proximity of victim

Milgram varied the proximity of the 'teacher' to the 'learner'. Obedience rates declined as the distance between them decreased, suggesting that distance made teachers oblivious to the consequences of their obedience, but physical presence and contact made teachers empathise more strongly with the learner's suffering, making it harder to deny or ignore.

Proximity of authority

In another variation, the experimenter left the room before the 'learning' session and continued to give instructions by telephone. In this condition, less than a quarter of participants went to the maximum shock level, showing that the authority's direct surveillance was a crucial factor in determining obedience in this setting.

Institutional context

Milgram's initial experiments took place in the prestigious location of Yale University. He carried out a follow-up study (under the guise of a fictional organisation called Research Associates of Bridgeport) in a run-down office building. In this study, less than half delivered the maximum shock, suggesting that reducing the perceived legitimacy of the surrounding organisation made a difference to obedience.

How people resist obedience

Reversing agentic shift

During the process of obedience, individuals shift the responsibility for their actions onto the authority figure. They can, however, be reminded that it is *they* who are responsible for their actions, not the authority figure. Hamilton (1978) found that under these conditions, agentic shift was reversed and sharp decreases in obedience could be obtained.

The role of disobedient models

The presence of **disobedient** models (which might suggest that obedience was inappropriate) can also serve to reduce obedience. In Milgram's research the presence of two disobedient peers was sufficient to override all the binding and agentic shift dynamics that usually produced an obedient response. The presence of 'rebels', therefore, helps the person see resistance as **legitimate**.

Critical issue: ethical issues in psychological research

Specification content

Ethical issues surrounding the use of deception, informed consent and the protection of participants from psychological harm, including the relevance of these issues in the context of social influence research. Ways in which psychologists deal with these issues (e.g. through the use of ethical guidelines).

Here you are expected to know about **ethical issues** of deception, informed consent and protection from psychological harm. *Why* are these such important issues in psychological research? This might involve looking at the potential damage caused by deceiving research participants or exposing them to stressful situations. These particular ethical issues have been chosen because they are important in social influence research, where they are particularly relevant to the work of **Milgram** and **Zimbardo**. You should, therefore, be able to demonstrate exactly how these issues surfaced during this research, and whether, in the light of such ethical concerns, such research could be justified.

Psychologists deal with ethical issues in various ways, but the most obvious way is through the development of **ethical guidelines**. You should know, in general terms, how the ethical guidelines are constructed and applied, and, specifically, how each of the three ethical issues mentioned previously are handled by these guidelines. Remember to *treat this area critically*, as you may be asked to evaluate the particular way of dealing with ethical issues that you have selected for your answer.

Ethical issues in psychological research

Deception
Deception can make participants suspicious about a research investigation, or they might develop negative feelings about taking part in any future research. It might reduce support for psychological research in general, and undermine the commitment of researchers to always tell the truth. The most serious consequence of deception is that it removes the ability of research participants to give their full informed consent to take part in an investigation. This creates dilemmas for the researcher, as complete openness might decrease the effectiveness of the investigation.

Informed consent
The principle of informed consent is that research participants should be allowed to agree or refuse to participate in the light of comprehensive information concerning the nature and purpose of the research. To be **informed** suggests that all relevant aspects of what is to happen and what *might* happen are disclosed to the participant and that they should be able to understand this information. **Consent** suggests that the participant is sufficiently competent to make a rational and mature judgement and that his/her agreement to participate should be voluntary, and free from coercion or undue influence.

Protection of participants from psychological harm
A further concern is that participants should be protected from undue risk during psychological research. The definition of undue risk is based on the risks that individuals might be expected to encounter in their normal lifestyle. Thus, the risks that an individual might be exposed to during a psychological investigation should not be greater than the risks they might already be expected to face in their everyday life.

Ethical issues and social influence research

Deception

Baumrind (1964) claimed that Milgram, in his study of obedience, had deceived his participants on two counts. First, he had led them to believe they were taking part in a study on the effects of punishment on learning. Second, he had then led them to believe they were actually delivering electric shocks. In Milgram's research, complete honesty would have made the research untenable. The justification for this conclusion comes from the fact that there was a large discrepancy between what was predicted *before* the study took place, and the *actual* findings.

Informed consent

For Milgram's study to work, deception was essential. This meant that, although his participants had given their permission to take part in a study on the relationship between punishment and learning, they had not given their consent to take part in a study of obedience to authority. Therefore, they had not given their informed consent to take part in this study. Baumrind claimed that Milgram took advantage of the trust of his participants, and exposed them to very high levels of stress — stress that they had not willingly agreed to experience. In defence of his procedures, Milgram claimed that he could not have foreseen the severity of the stress experienced by his participants (Milgram, 1974).

Protection of participants from psychological harm

Baumrind criticised Milgram's study on the basis that participants would suffer permanent psychological harm, including a loss of dignity, self-esteem and trust of authority (Baumrind, 1964). She also suggested that Milgram had not done enough to remove any of the trauma the participants had felt after taking part in the study. Milgram responded by showing that all his participants had been thoroughly debriefed at the end of the study. He also provided evidence that in psychiatric examinations 1 year after the study, there was no sign of any psychological damage directly attributable to the experiment. Milgram claimed that most criticisms arose because of the *results* of the study rather than the *procedures* used.

Dealing with ethical issues

Ethical guidelines

Ethical guidelines help to guide conduct within a particular profession, and establish guidelines for standard practice and competence. The 'role' of ethical guidelines is summarised in the *BPS Code of Conduct* (1993): 'to preserve an overriding high regard for the well-being and dignity of research participants'.

Ethical guidelines tend to be based on a 'cost–benefit' approach in that scientific ends are sometimes seen as justifying the use of methods that sometimes sacrifice participants' welfare, particularly when the research promises 'the greatest good for the greatest number' (the utilitarian argument).

Each section of the BPS guidelines consists of a series of statements clarifying appropriate conduct (e.g. consent, deception and protection of participants).

Consent

Whenever possible, the investigators should inform all participants of the objectives of the investigation and all aspects of the research or intervention that might reasonably be expected to influence willingness to participate. Research with children or with participants who have impairments that limit understanding and/or communication, such that they are unable to give their real consent, requires special safeguarding procedures.

Deception

The withholding of information or the misleading of participants is unacceptable if the participants are likely to show unease once debriefed. Where this is in any doubt, appropriate consultation must precede the investigation. Intentional deception of the participants over the purpose and general nature of the investigation should be avoided whenever possible.

Protection of participants

Investigators have a primary responsibility to protect participants from physical and mental harm during the investigation. Normally the risk of harm must be no greater than in ordinary life. Where research might involve behaviour or experiences that participants could regard as personal and private, the participants must be protected from stress by all appropriate measures, including the assurance that answers to personal questions need not be given.

Evaluation

- Most professional codes, particularly those in the social sciences, have very little power of censure over their members, although the BPS Chartered Psychologist status does go some way to controlling the activities of members of the profession. Exclusion from a professional body does not prevent social scientists from continuing to carry out research.
- Ethical guidelines might protect the immediate needs of research participants, but might not deal with all the possible ways in which research can inflict harm on a group of people or section of society (e.g. members of a particular racial, gender or sexual group). The Canadian Psychological Association, however, advises its members to 'analyse likely short-term, ongoing, and long-term risks and benefits of each course of action on the individual(s)/group(s) involved or likely to be affected'.

Social psychology: defining the terms

conformity/majority influence: conformity is a form of social influence that results from exposure to the opinions of a majority. It is the tendency for people to adopt the behaviour, attitudes and values of other members of a reference group.

deception: the withholding of information or the misleading of research participants. A distinction is usually made between withholding some details of the research hypothesis, and deliberately providing false information to participants that might influence their willingness to take part.

ecological validity: a measure of whether the findings of a study could be generalised to other situations and settings. If a laboratory investigation lacks ecological validity, it usually means that some aspect of the study is not appropriate in another context and therefore conclusions drawn from it might not be justified.

ethical guidelines: concrete, quasi-legal documents that help to guide conduct within psychology by establishing guidelines for standard practice and competence.

ethical issue: an ethical issue arises in research when there are conflicting sets of values concerning the goals, procedures or outcomes of a research study. For example, researchers must weigh up the importance of gaining full informed consent from participants, against the scientific importance of observing behaviour as it occurs naturally in different social settings.

experimental validity: a measure of whether the experimental procedures really worked, and therefore whether the observed effect was caused by the experimental manipulation. The degree to which an experiment has high levels of experimental validity determines whether the conclusions of a study are justified.

informed consent: the right of research participants to agree or refuse to participate in a research investigation, based on receiving comprehensive information concerning the nature and purpose of the research.

minority influence: a form of social influence whereby people reject the established norm of the majority of group members and move to the position of the minority.

obedience to authority: a type of social influence whereby someone acts in response to a direct order from another person. There is also the implication that the person receiving the order is made to respond in a way that they would not otherwise have done without the order.

protection of participants from psychological harm: an ethical guideline which states that research participants should be protected from undue risk during an investigation. This might include embarrassment, loss of dignity or threats to a person's self-esteem as a result of participation.

social influence: the various processes (such as majority and minority influence) by which a person's attitudes, beliefs and behaviours are modified by the presence or actions of others.

Research methods

It is anticipated that some of the material for this section of Module 3 will be taught in association with other modules.

Be prepared to use your knowledge from other modules or from the other section of this module to help you understand this Research Methods section. For example, the information on social influence in the first part of this guide illustrates the application of ethical guidelines; research in many other areas illustrates the methods included here and their advantages and weaknesses.

Quantitative and qualitative research methods

Specification content

The nature and usage of the following research methods, their advantages and weaknesses and how they relate to the scientific nature of psychology.
- *experiments (including laboratory, field and natural experiments)*
- *investigations using correlational analysis*
- *naturalistic observation*
- *questionnaire surveys*
- *interviews*

The nature and usage of ethical guidelines in psychology.

You need to be able to describe briefly each of the methods listed and know how they are used in psychological research. For each method you should know at least two advantages and two weaknesses (note the use of the plurals in the specification). You should also appreciate that all the methods have an important place in psychological research. Do not fall into the trap of thinking that laboratory experiments alone are scientific and criticise other methods for not being as 'good'. All methods can be used in a scientific or unscientific manner, depending on the skill of the researcher. Finally, you should know about ethical guidelines in psychological research and how to apply them appropriately.

Research methods and their advantages and weaknesses

Experiments (including laboratory, field and natural experiments)

An experiment is a research method in which the experimenter manipulates something that influences the participants (an **independent variable** or **IV**) and observes and measures the effects of the changes on their behaviour (the **dependent** variable or **DV**) while keeping all other sources of influence (**extraneous variables**) constant. Experiments enable researchers to look for *differences* between two conditions and so detect **cause-and-effect** relationships.

- In a **laboratory experiment** the experimenter has direct control over both the IV and the research setting.
- In a **field experiment** the experimenter has direct control over the IV but the setting is a naturally occurring one which is familiar ('home ground') to participants.
- In a **quasi experiment** the experimenter has no direct control over the IV. (It occurs **fortuitously** — by good fortune.) The research setting, however, is under the experimenter's control.
- In a **natural experiment** the experimenter has *no* direct control over the IV or the research setting. Both occur fortuitously.

Advantages of experiments

- The rigorous control possible, particularly in the laboratory experiment, makes it possible for the experimenter to make causal statements about behaviour.
- Knowing what causes changes in behaviour raises the possibility of being able to change or control it.

Weaknesses of experiments

- In spite of rigorous control, there is always the chance that behaviour is not affected by the IV but by a **confounding variable** — an unwanted and systematic influence on the DV that has not been properly controlled. The relatively weaker control over variables in the more 'true-to-life' experiments, such as the natural experiment, means that the experimenter can be even less confident in conclusions about cause.
- Rigorous control in certain kinds of experiment, especially the laboratory experiment, has invited the criticism that such research can be **reductionist** and so loses sight of the complexity of behaviour in 'real-life' settings.

Investigations using correlational analysis

Correlation is not a research method in itself. It is a *technique of data analysis* that is especially useful for detecting patterns in data. It is particularly useful when experimental manipulation is inappropriate or not possible. To apply correlation, it is necessary to collect scores that are *paired*, for example personality scores and self-esteem scores, or hours viewing certain television programmes and tendency to behave in a pro-social way. Correlation is used to detect a **linear relationship** between these samples of paired data.

Correlation can be expressed visually as a **scattergraph**, or numerically as a **correlation coefficient** which ranges from +1 through 0 to –1. The sign (+ or –) indicates the direction of the relationship; the number (0 to 1) gives the strength of the relationship. For example, the correlation coefficients +0.6 and +0.7 are both positive but +0.6 is the weaker of the two; correlation coefficients of +0.7 and –0.7 are the same strength, but different in direction.

Advantages of investigations using correlational analysis
- Correlation allows us to see how two variables relate to each other. For example, a positive relationship between summer temperatures and ice-cream sales indicates that high temperatures are related to high sales and low temperatures to low sales.
- It enables us to predict the likely value of one variable when we only have information about the other.

Weaknesses of investigations using correlational analysis
- Correlation is a description of relationships between variables. It does not allow us to say one variable causes changes in another. For example, there may be a positive relationship between hours spent watching certain kinds of television programme and pro-social behaviour, but this does not mean one causes the other. Other factors could be involved.
- Important relationships between two variables can sometimes be curvilinear. Simple correlational analysis is unable to pick this up. Care must therefore be taken to examine the scattergraph to ensure that it shows an appropriate linear pattern.

Naturalistic observation
Observational methods involve the researcher in systematically watching and recording behaviour in order to be able to *describe* it. The term **naturalistic** means that the observation is made in a setting that is familiar to participants, for example, home, a school-room or a public place.

Advantages of naturalistic observation
- Naturalistic observation can produce rich and detailed descriptive accounts of behaviour.
- It can be used when other methods might be impractical or unethical. For example, we cannot manipulate the type of parenting experienced by children but we can observe existing patterns of parenting along with children's behaviour.

Weaknesses of naturalistic observation
- If the observer's presence is obvious, it could affect participants' behaviour in unwanted ways. If it is not made obvious, ethical issues, such as inability of the observer to obtain informed consent or debrief participants, are raised.
- There are many uncontrolled influences that could affect participants' observed behaviour, making it difficult to decide which are the important ones.

Questionnaire surveys
A **survey** is usually a large-scale study of a **representative sample** of a particular **population**'s attitudes, opinions or behaviour patterns. When **questionnaires** are used to collect this information we have a **questionnaire survey**. Questionnaires usually comprise a standard set of questions about an issue or topic and are presented to all participants in exactly the same way, for example, face-to-face, by post or by telephone.

Questionnaires can be used to tap into many aspects of respondents' lives. For example, they can be used to gather **factual** and **demographic** information. Psychologists are more likely to be interested in connecting these variables with such things as behaviour patterns, attitudes and beliefs, knowledge, intentions or aspirations.

Advantages of questionnaire surveys
- Questionnaire surveys are useful for collecting relatively large amounts of information quickly and efficiently. For example, they can be completed independently by the participant.
- In certain questionnaire surveys, assuring the respondents of anonymity, or using a method not involving face-to-face contact with the researcher, can encourage more honest responses. Respondents might feel freed from the need to give a socially favourable impression.

Weaknesses of questionnaire surveys
- When respondents can be identified in surveys, they may alter their true responses to give a socially favourable impression, thus distorting the results.
- Good sampling is essential if the results are to be generalisable to the population from which the sample was drawn. Unfortunately, questionnaire surveys typically have low rates of return, so generalisation needs to be made with great skill and care. For example, respondents may participate because they are interested in the issues being surveyed. The sample thus becomes 'self-selected'.

Interviews
Interviews are usually carried out one-to-one, with face-to-face contact between researcher and interviewee. They generally yield richer written data than can be obtained from questionnaires. Interviews can be structured, semi-structured or clinical (see page 29).

Advantages of interviews
- Interviews can provide more complex and detailed information than other methods, and avoid criticisms of reductionism.
- Information can be gained about the individual's subjective view. This is useful if the researcher feels it is inappropriate to impose his/her own way of viewing something upon the participant and wishes to allow flexibility of response.

Weaknesses of interviews
- Interviews tend to yield information that is open to misinterpretation, over-interpretation or partial interpretation, because of biases on the researcher's part.
- If the issue to be explored is personal or otherwise sensitive, the interviewee may not be totally open and honest.

The nature and usage of ethical guidelines in psychology

Ethics are **moral standards** and **rules of conduct**. The British Psychological Society (BPS) has devised, and regularly updates, *Ethical Principles for Conducting*

Research with Human Participants, to guide research psychologists. The BPS also has an ethics committee, to which possible breaches of the code of conduct can be referred. Pages 18–21 describe ethical issues concerning **consent**, **deception** and **protection of participants** and explain how they can be dealt with. These issues are relevant in all the psychological research methods described in this section.

Research design and implementation

Specification content

- *Aims and hypotheses (including the generation of appropriate aims; the formulation of different types of experimental/alternative hypothesis (directional/non-directional), and the null hypothesis).*
- *Research designs: experimental (including independent groups, repeated measures and matched participants); and the design of naturalistic observations, questionnaire surveys and interviews.*
- *Factors associated with research design, including the operationalisation of the IV/DV; conducting pilot studies; control of variables; techniques for assessing and improving reliability and validity (internal and external (ecological) validity); ethics.*
- *The selection of participants (including random sampling).*
- *The relationship between researchers and participants (including demand characteristics and investigator effects).*

Here you are required to know how to word different kinds of hypothesis. Understanding techniques for good research design is also important. You should know how to set up the research designs listed, why certain designs are chosen over others and how to avoid pitfalls that lead to poor design. You should be able to name types of reliability and validity and know how to assess and improve them. Ethics are important here too, as in the previous section. Know what 'random sampling' means and at least two other ways of selecting research participants. You should also be able to explain how researchers and participants can affect each other's behaviour and how you can minimise the problems this could cause.

Aims and hypotheses

Research studies usually begin with a **question** based on research or theory, which research **aims** to answer. For example, 'is the performance of female students in an exam affected by the sex of the invigilator?' In certain kinds of research, this is re-phrased to make a **hypothesis** — a statement about the outcome of a statistically testable study. For example, 'there is a difference in the mean exam scores of female students depending upon whether the exam is invigilated by a male or a female'. This is an **experimental hypothesis** because it states that there is a *difference* in mean scores under the two conditions.

Correlational hypotheses state that there is a *relationship*. For example, 'there is a relationship between personality scores on test X and self-esteem scores on test Y'. Hypotheses for χ^2 analysis predict an association or, sometimes, a difference. For example, 'there is an association between drivers' sex and whether or not they obey a stop sign'.

Directional hypotheses state the direction of a difference (for example, 'girls' spelling is superior to that of boys') or correlation (for example, 'there is a positive relationship between weight and height'). **Non-directional hypotheses** allow for differences or correlation in either direction (for example, 'there is a difference in...' or 'there is a correlation between...'). Hypotheses for χ^2 are usually non-directional.

For these hypotheses there is always a **null hypothesis**, which states that there is no difference between scores under the two conditions compared in an experiment (or no correlation or association between the two variables of interest). If research results enable us to reject the null hypothesis, we can retain the **alternative hypothesis** which states that there is a difference (or correlation or association, depending on the design of the investigation), which can be directional or non-directional.

Research designs

Experiments

Simple, two-sample experiments usually have:
- a **control group**, which is not affected by the IV and provides baseline data
- an **experimental group**, which is influenced by the IV

In some experiments two levels of the IV are compared if the IV cannot be eliminated from one condition. There are three experimental designs used to control **variation due to participants**:

The independent groups design

A sample of participants is randomly allocated between the two conditions, or the groups occur naturally. **Random allocation** should balance out differences between participants. This design is relatively quick and easy to set up and avoids order effects. However, it uses more participants than the repeated measures design, and differences between the two groups will probably be greater at the outset than in the following two designs.

The repeated measures design

Participants take part in both conditions, so this design is economical with participant numbers. Individual differences across conditions are minimised, but **order effects** are more likely (participants may carry over the effects of practice or fatigue from one condition to the other). **Randomised presentation** of conditions can minimise this, as can **counterbalancing**, in which half the participants do condition A first and half do B first (ABBA design). A further problem is that participants may not return to be tested a second time and so are lost from the study.

The matched pairs design

Participants are paired on the basis of relevant variables. For example, in a test of the effects of alcohol intake on driving ability, participants could be matched for age, body weight, driving experience and usual drinking pattern. One member of the pair is then randomly assigned to condition A and the other to condition B. Individual differences between conditions are controlled to some extent, although some will remain uncontrolled. The problem of order effects does not occur. However, good matching can be difficult and more participants are needed than in the repeated measures design. Also, loss of one person results in the loss of a pair of data.

Naturalistic observations

In naturalistic observation, the researcher might observe and record participants' behaviour in a natural setting, either from the outside (**non-participant observation**) or from within the group (**participant observation**). Observations differ in how focused or general they are, their time-scale and structure. The method of data collection can vary from simple frequency counts to sophisticated recording techniques. Data can be in the form of notes, written transcripts, checklists, tallies or video or audio recordings. Sometimes **behaviour traces** can be observed — for example, in studies of littering. Alternatively, **archival data** can be examined — for example, diaries or other records. Ethical considerations about **informed consent** and respect for the **rights** and **privacy** of participants are especially important in naturalistic observation, as is the issue of maximising **reliability** of observations.

Questionnaire surveys

These have two important elements:

- good questionnaire design
- adequate sampling

The design of a good questionnaire is a lengthy and skilled business. Questions can be **open** (allowing more detailed and flexible responses) or **closed** (where respondents have to choose from a set of fixed-choice answers). Great care must be taken to avoid questions that are ambiguous, 'lead' the respondent or cause offence. For notes on sampling, see pages 31–32.

Interviews

Interviews usually take one of three forms:

- **structured** — questions are fixed and the participant chooses from fixed answers
- **semi-structured** — some fixed questions may also be necessary, but generally questions are worded more openly, and flexibility is allowed in responses (the interviewer might build in prompts to obtain more information and keep the interview on course, and may vary the order of questioning)
- **unstructured** — the interviewer has a topic in mind but allows the interviewee to decide what issues to raise and discuss in relation to this topic

Care must be taken to relax the interviewees and to ensure that they do not feel constrained from expressing themselves honestly. **Ethical considerations** of participants' rights, confidentiality, protection and consent are especially important.

Factors associated with research design

Operationalising variables

In certain kinds of research (e.g. experiments), it is necessary to define precisely (**operationalise**) what the variables used in hypotheses mean, so that they are measurable (**quantifiable**). This can be problematic with concepts such as aggression or anxiety, but less so with others. For example, in a study investigating the hypothesis that fatigue impairs memory, fatigue might be operationalised as number of hours slept in the preceding week, while memory might be operationalised as number of words recalled from a previously memorised list.

Pilot studies

With any type of research it is good practice to carry out a small-scale 'dry run' or pilot study. This usually enables the researcher to identify any problems with such things as clarity of instructions or questions, timing, appropriateness of measures or recording of responses. Problems can then be corrected in advance of the main study.

Control of variables

Single-blind procedure

Participants are not informed of the research aim or hypothesis. This helps to ensure that **participant reactivity** (see page 31) is minimised.

Double-blind procedure

The researcher instructs someone else to collect the data but does not let that person or the participants know the hypothesis. This helps to minimise **investigator effects** and **participant reactivity**.

Standardised instructions and conditions

The researcher ensures that instructions are given in the same way for all participants in a particular condition. **Testing conditions** should also be the same for all participants in a particular condition. These procedures aim to avoid favouring some participants over others.

Techniques for assessing and improving reliability and validity

Reliability means consistency — a test or research study is reliable if it can be depended upon to produce the same, or similar, results every time it is carried out. This can often be checked using correlation. **Inter-observer reliability** is assessed when two or more observers check their observations to see if there is agreement. **Intra-observer reliability** is assessed when the same observer makes repeated observations which are checked against each other to see if there is agreement. **Test–retest reliability** is assessed when a test or other procedure produces similar results on two or more occasions.

Validity means **relevance** or **appropriateness**. **Internal validity** refers to the internal 'worth' of any research, i.e. that it really is measuring what it is supposed to measure. Careful research design and/or rigorous controls should ensure that there are no biases or other design problems interfering with this. **Experimental validity** is one form of internal validity and is evident if we can be confident that an IV in an experiment really was responsible for changes in a DV. **External validity** is assessed by testing to see whether the research findings can also be observed outside the original research situation, when applied to either different groups of people (**population validity**), situations (**ecological validity**) or time periods (**temporal validity**).

The selection of participants

Populations and samples

In psychological research, a **population** is the total number of individuals who are eligible to participate because they have certain characteristics, for example, all AS psychology students in a particular county in a particular year. Usually, a representative group, called a **sample**, is selected from the population. The sample should be large enough to represent the population adequately.

Sampling procedures are used because:
- it may only be **practical** to study a fraction of the population
- they help to ensure that the sample is **representative** of the population
- findings from a representative sample can be **generalised** to the population from which the sample was drawn

Types of sampling

In **random sampling**, individual members of a population are assigned an identifier, such as a number, and the required number of participants is then selected using random number tables or computer-generated random numbers. Each member of the population has an *equal chance* of being chosen. **Stratified random sampling** is used when the population has important sub-groups (strata). Random samples are taken from each stratum in the same proportions that exist in the population. In **opportunity sampling**, the researcher decides on the type of participant needed and approaches anyone who appears suitable until sufficient numbers have been obtained. In **quota sampling**, the population is organised into sub-groups (strata) and opportunity samples are taken from each stratum in the same proportions that appear in the population.

The relationship between researchers and participants

In any research situation, participants might respond to **demand characteristics**. These are cues in the research situation, such as the way the study is set up or the researcher's behaviour, that might alert the participants to the hypothesis being tested or otherwise make them feel they should behave in particular ways. Demand characteristics might lead to **participant reactivity** which could be a source of unwanted influence on the research outcome.

Faithful participants try to react to the situation as naturally as possible, but:
- a **cooperative** participant tries to find out the purpose of the study so he/she can help to support it
- a **negativistic** participant tries to discover the purpose of the study in order to work against it
- an **evaluatively apprehensive** participant worries about the impression created by what the experimenter might find out about him/her

It is also important to guard against **investigator effects**. Researchers who have a particular aim or hypothesis in mind might unconsciously influence how their findings turn out. Single- and double-blind procedures can help to guard against both participant reactivity and investigator effects.

Data analysis

Specification content

- *Analysis of qualitative data that could be derived from naturalistic observations, questionnaire surveys and interviews.*
- *Measures of central tendency and dispersion (including the appropriate use and interpretation of medians, means, modes, range and standard deviations).*
- *The nature of positive and negative correlations and the interpretation of correlation coefficients.*
- *Graphs and charts (including the appropriate use and interpretation of histograms, bar charts, frequency polygons and scattergraphs).*

Here you need to show that you can choose and utilise appropriate techniques of analysis for both qualitative and quantitative data. You should know all the descriptive statistics of central tendency and dispersion listed, and how to apply them correctly. You should be able to recognise and interpret positive and negative correlation coefficients. Finally, you need to know about the appropriate use of 'visual' forms of descriptive data presentation, and how to interpret these data.

Analysis of qualitative data

Qualitative data collected from naturalistic observations, questionnaire surveys or interviews take many forms. These include:
- written records of events, e.g. field notes or interview transcripts
- video or audio recordings
- coding or checklists, e.g. frequencies of occurrences of certain events
- behaviour traces, e.g. degree of littering

These can be analysed **qualitatively**, **quantitatively**, or both, depending on the type of data collected. Qualitative analysis of purely textual data usually involves making a written transcript and examining it in detail for recurrent **themes** and **meanings**. Evidence for each of these is gathered from the text so that they can be discussed in turn. Studies yielding frequency data can be treated using **descriptive statistics** such as **percentages**, or presented illustratively in **bar graphs**. Text can also be subjected to **content analysis** in which categories are set up so that the frequency of occurrence of particular kinds of statement can be counted. These frequencies can then be presented as percentages or in bar graphs.

Measures of central tendency and dispersion

Measures of central tendency

These are used for summarising large amounts of data into one typical, or average, value. Such measures include:

- the **mean**, which is the sum of scores divided by the number of scores
- the **median**, which is the central score in a list of rank-ordered scores
- the **mode**, which is the most frequently occurring value in a set of scores

The median is preferred to the mean when the distribution of scores is **skewed** as a result of there being a small number of atypical scores (which can be either high or low). The mean is easily distorted by such scores but the median is not affected by them. The mode is also immune to extreme scores and is additionally useful for summarising large samples of **similar data** and data in **bi-** or **multi-modal distributions**.

Measures of dispersion

These are used to indicate the amount of variability, or spread, in a sample of scores. They include:

- the **standard deviation**, which is obtained by calculating the amount by which each score in a sample differs (deviates) from the sample mean and then finding the amount by which the scores *typically* differ from the mean. Around 68% of the scores in the sample fall within ±1SD from the mean.
- the **range**, which is obtained by finding the difference between the highest and lowest scores in a sample of scores

Correlations and correlation coefficients

A **positive** correlation indicates that as scores on one variable increase, so do their partner scores on the other variable. A **negative** correlation indicates that as scores on one variable increase, their partner scores on the other variable decrease.

Correlation analysis will reveal one of the following patterns:

- **perfect positive correlation**, +1.0 (e.g. number of pounds spent and number of items purchased worth 50p each). A correlation of +1.0 is rare in psychological research.

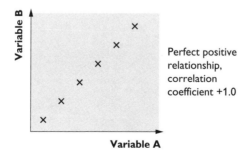

Perfect positive relationship, correlation coefficient +1.0

- **imperfect positive correlation**, for example +0.7 (e.g. number of hours spent revising and end-of-course grades)

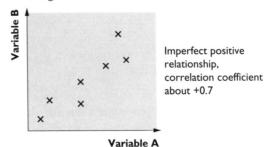

Imperfect positive relationship, correlation coefficient about +0.7

- **no correlation**, 0 (e.g. shoe size and number of pets owned)

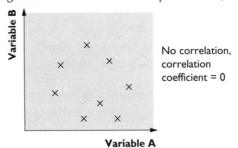

No correlation, correlation coefficient = 0

- **imperfect negative correlation**, for example –0.6 (e.g. number of hours spent socialising during a course and end-of-term grades)

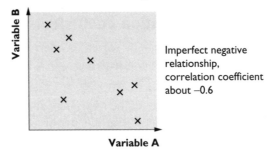

Imperfect negative relationship, correlation coefficient about –0.6

- **perfect negative correlation**, –1.0 (e.g. heights of a group of people and their distance from the same ceiling). A correlation of –1.0 is rare in psychological research.

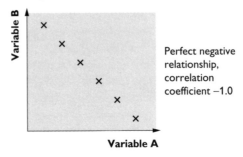

Perfect negative relationship, correlation coefficient –1.0

Graphs and charts

The correct use of graphs and charts depends on the kind of measurement scale the researcher has used when collecting the data:

- **nominal data** — frequency counts into named categories, for example number of males and females in specified categories
- **ordinal data** — values on a ranked scale, for example attractiveness ratings
- **interval or ratio data** — values represent a point on a more sophisticated measurement scale, for example IQ points or physical measurements (e.g. reaction time in milliseconds)

Bar charts

Bar charts are used to show frequencies in nominal and ordinal data, but they can also be used to show means or percentages. Frequency, mean or percentage is plotted on the vertical axis and the measurement scale is plotted on the horizontal axis. Bar charts are drawn:

- with gaps between the bars
- with categories in alphabetical order (nominal data)
- using naturally occurring order (ordinal data)

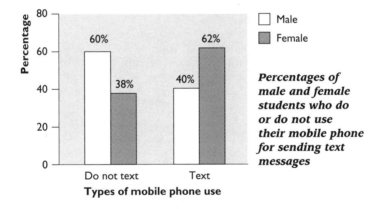

Percentages of male and female students who do or do not use their mobile phone for sending text messages

Histograms and frequency polygons

These are used to show frequencies in interval and ratio data. Such data can be:

- **discrete** — whole units are more meaningful and are not usually divided down ad infinitum, for example numbers of children in families
- **continuous** — in theory, such data can be divided down ad infinitum, for example time can be divided down into smaller and smaller units

Frequency is plotted on the vertical axis and the measurement scale is plotted on the horizontal axis.

In histograms:

- discrete data are usually appropriate
- bars always represent frequencies
- bars touch each other

- all values must be shown, even if they are zero
- the area represented by the bars is mathematically meaningful

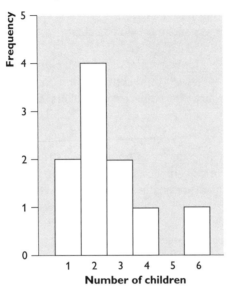

Total number of children in a sample of ten 12-year-olds' families

In frequency polygons:
- continuous data are usually appropriate
- apply the same rules as for histograms, except that the midpoints of class intervals (divisions of the scale) are joined by a continuous line
- the area underneath the curve is mathematically meaningful

In practice, you will see both histograms and frequency polygons for discrete and continuous data. It's a 'foggy' area.

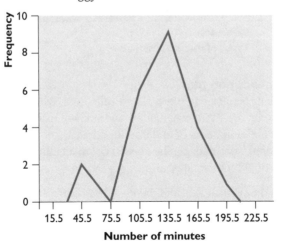

Number of minutes per school night spent doing homework by Y12 students

Scattergraphs
These are used to represent visually the extent of correlation between two variables.

They are used to indicate:
- the direction of a relationship
- whether there are any outliers or otherwise unusual scores
- whether the relationship really is linear (rather than curvilinear)

One variable is plotted on the vertical axis and the other on the horizontal axis. Each pair of scores is represented by one point on the scattergraph, rather like coordinates on a map. The direction *and* strength of a relationship can be tested by calculating a correlation coefficient.

Research methods: defining the terms

bar chart: a visual means of showing frequencies, means or percentages in nominal or ordinal data.

central tendency: a statistical measure used for summarising large amounts of data into one typical or average value, for example mean, median or mode.

confounding variable: an uncontrolled variable that exerts an unwanted, systematic effect on a dependent variable.

correlational analysis: a method of data analysis used to detect linear relationships between samples of paired data.

demand characteristics: cues in a research situation that participants might interpret as indicating that they should behave in a particular way.

dispersion: a statistical measure used to indicate the amount of spread or variability in a sample of data, for example range or standard deviation.

double-blind procedure: for example control technique in which both participants and the investigator collecting the data do not know the purpose of the study. This helps to guard against participant reactivity and investigator effects.

experiment: a research technique in which an investigator manipulates an IV and observes and measures corresponding changes in a DV, while keeping extraneous variables constant.

frequency polygon: a visual means of showing frequencies in continuous, interval or ratio data.

histogram: a visual means of showing frequencies in discrete interval or ratio data.

hypothesis: a statement about the outcome of a statistically testable research study.

investigator effects: the unwanted, and usually unconscious, influence that the investigator's beliefs about the outcome of a research study may have on the results.

naturalistic observation: a research method that involves watching and recording participants' behaviour in a setting that is familiar to them.

operationalisation: a precise definition of terms used in a research study that enables them to be measured (or quantified).

participant reactivity: the unwanted, and sometimes unconscious, influence that the participants' beliefs about, or attitudes towards, a research study may have over how they behave in it.

pilot study: a small-scale 'dry run' of a proposed research study which is used to identify problems and correct them before the main study is conducted.

population: the total number of individuals who are eligible to participate in a research study because they have particular characteristics. (To be more exact, the term 'population' refers to a population of data rather than of people.)

questionnaire survey: a large-scale study in which a representative sample of individuals is taken from a population and information gathered from them by means of a questionnaire.

reliability: consistency of research findings between observers (inter-observer reliability), within an observer (intra-observer reliability) or between testing occasions (test–retest reliability).

sample: a group of people (or sample of data) selected from a population in such a way that it is representative of the population. Findings from a representative sample can be generalised to the population.

scattergraph: a visual means of showing whether there is a linear relationship (correlation) between samples of paired data.

single-blind procedure: a control technique in which participants do not know the purpose of the study. This helps to guard against participant reactivity.

validity: the relevance or appropriateness of a research study. A well-designed study has internal validity, e.g. experimental validity. External validity can be checked by seeing whether findings transfer to different settings (ecological validity) or different people (population validity).

Questions
&
Answers

In this section of the guide there are six questions — four on Social Psychology and two on Research Methods. Each question is worth 30 marks and would be answered in 30 minutes. It is important to divide your time, when answering examination questions such as these, according to the mark allocation for each part.

The section is structured as follows:

- sample questions in the style of the unit
- example candidate responses at the B- or C-grade level (candidate A) — these will demonstrate both strengths and weaknesses of responses with potential for improvement
- example candidate responses at the A-grade level (candidate B) — such answers demonstrate thorough knowledge, a good understanding and an ability to deal with the data that are presented in the questions

Examiner's comments

All candidate responses are followed by examiner's comments. These are preceded by the icon 🖉. They indicate where credit is due. In the weaker answers, they also point out areas for improvement, specific problems and common errors such as poor time management, lack of clarity, weak or non-existent development, irrelevance, misinterpretation of the question and mistaken meanings of terms.

The comments also indicate how each example answer would have been marked in an actual exam, using the criteria listed on pages 7–8.

Social psychology (I)

(a) **What is meant by the terms 'obedience to authority', 'ecological validity'**
    and 'informed consent'?   (2+2+2 marks)
(b) **Outline two reasons why people obey.**   (3 + 3 marks)
(c) **'Laboratory studies of obedience are rarely convincing, either in the**
    deception of participants, or their ability to explain obedience in the real world.'
    Consider whether such criticisms of the validity of obedience research are
    justified.   (18 marks)

                                                          Total: 30 marks

(a) These three terms can each be defined using the definitions on page 22. You are
    not *required* to offer such elaborate definitions, but the more accurate and detailed
    your definition, the more likely it is that you will pick up the full 2 marks offered.

(b) As this question asks for *two* reasons why people obey, it is important to
    remember that these are marked independently, so don't spend a disproportionate
    amount of time on one rather than the other. Try to put yourself in the shoes of
    the examiner, who must have some way of discriminating between the level of
    accuracy and detail necessary for a 1-, 2- or 3-mark response. If you are stuck for
    detail, try giving an example.

(c) This part constitutes the AO1 + AO2 component of the question. Although you
    are not required to reach a definite conclusion, you are required to engage with
    the material in a critical and analytic manner. Orne and Holland criticised the
    validity of Milgram's research into obedience on several counts, yet Milgram
    provided a robust defence in return. Being aware of this debate, and being able to
    examine the claims of both sides in a searching and critical manner, would
    constitute an appropriate response to this question.

■ ■ ■

Answer to question 1: candidate A

(a) Obedience means doing what you are told by someone else in authority.
    Ecological validity is when research is carried out in the natural environment;
    it means true to life rather than being artificial.
    Informed consent is when you tell someone everything they need to know
    about an experiment before they take part. That way they can make a decision
    based on that information rather than just agreeing without having enough infor-
    mation about what they're letting themselves in for.

There is enough in the first answer for 1 mark (this is a largely common-sense
    definition) but it lacks the detail necessary for the full 2 marks. There is some
    accuracy in the second answer, but it too lacks the precision necessary for the
    2 marks. Although research in the natural environment does tend to have higher

levels of ecological validity, the term 'ecological validity' means more than just 'true to life'. The third answer is accurate and contains enough detail for full marks. (4 out of 6 marks)

(b) One of the most important processes in obedience is agentic shift, which means that people simply shift their responsibility to another person so that they are not to blame for what happens. Another reason why people obey is because the person giving orders has authority and people are used to accepting what someone in authority tells them. As a result of this, they don't question that authority, and do what they are told to do. When we are young we are often told what to do by parents, teachers and even the police. We tend not to question this because they are a lot bigger and more important than us. As we get older, and gain more status, we should be able to resist authority figures, but we have grown used to obeying them and so find it hard to change.

> There are two explanations of why people obey — agentic shift and socialisation. Agentic shift in this context is more to do with the shift of responsibility onto the authority figure rather than simply 'another person'. There is a rather protracted explanation of socialisation effects, which is accurate nonetheless. This answer might have been improved by considering other reasons why we obey rather than adding all the unnecessary elaboration to this latter one. This answer is limited but generally accurate. (2 out of 3 marks for each reason — in total, 4 out of 6)

(c) Milgram's study of obedience deceived his participants on two main counts. First of all, he deceived them by not telling them what the study was really about. Participants volunteered for a study of the effects of punishment on learning, but it was actually a study of the effects of authority on obedience; they were the subject of the study, not the learner. The second way in which he deceived his participants was when he drew lots to see who would be the teacher and who would be the learner. This was rigged so that the real participant was always the teacher and the confederate of the experimenter was always the learner who received the electric shocks.

Critics have suggested that participants must have been suspicious about whether they really were giving electric shocks, although Milgram claimed that they showed surprise when they were led into the other room and saw that the learner was really unharmed. This criticism highlights a serious problem for this research, since if the deception didn't work (and the participants knew they weren't really shocking the learner), then the results would not be as valuable. Other critics of the validity of this research have claimed that it wasn't true to real life since it was carried out in a university laboratory. It is possible that participants might have been behaving in that way because they were in a university and would not have acted like that in a more natural setting.

Milgram repeated the experiment in some run-down offices and again got high levels of obedience, far higher than were predicted prior to the study beginning. This suggests that the obedience that Milgram discovered in his research did have some validity and was therefore relevant to behaviour in the real world.

📝 The first part of this answer picks up on the word 'deception' in the quotation, and embarks on an irrelevant discussion of the ways in which Milgram deceived his participants. This is *not* what is required by the question. Although the quotation is there to guide you towards a consideration of the issues involved, it is the *question* itself that has to be answered. When the answer finally does get going, it is reasonable in the way it addresses problems of experimental and ecological validity, although more could have been made of this material. The AO1 material (description of the criticisms themselves) is fairly limited and receives 3 of the 6 marks available for the AO1 component of this question. The AO2 material is limited, but has been used reasonably effectively. It does contain brief coverage of Milgram's defence of the validity of his findings, and does attempt to engage with the material in an 'AO2' manner. This pushes it towards 6 out of 12 marks for the AO2 component of this question.

Total for this question: 17 out of 30 marks

■ ■ ■

Answer to question 1: candidate B

📝 The following answer is supported by material presented earlier in this book and is equivalent to a good grade-A response to this question.

(a) Obedience to authority refers to a type of social influence whereby somebody acts in response to a direct order from another person. There is also the implication that the person receiving the order is made to respond in a way that they would not otherwise have done without the order.

The ecological validity of a study is a measure of whether the findings could be generalised out to other situations and settings. If a laboratory investigation lacks ecological validity, it usually means that some aspect of the study is not appropriate and therefore conclusions drawn from it might not be justified. Thus, it is also said to lack experimental validity.

Informed consent allows research participants to agree or refuse to participate in a research investigation, based on receiving comprehensive information concerning the nature and purpose of the research.

(b) In obedience experiments, binding factors appear to operate. Various cues (such as the experimenter's status and manner and the volunteer status of the participant) increase the pressure on the participant to continue. The participant is also able to shift the responsibility for his/her actions onto another person (the authority figure) through the process of agentic shift. They now see themselves as the agents of another person (the authority figure) and no longer responsible for their own actions. In Milgram's original study, the teacher and learner were in different rooms, with the teacher protected (i.e. buffered) from having to see their 'victim' and also from the consequences of the electric shocks. When the learner was in the same room, this buffer effect was reduced, as was the tendency to obey the commands of the experimenter, and therefore the overall level of obedience.

(c) Orne and Holland (1968) claimed that Milgram's obedience research lacked experimental validity and therefore the conclusions drawn from the study were inappropriate. According to this claim, participants had not *believed* that they were giving electric shocks, and pretended to be distressed as part of their 'role' in the experiment. Milgram defended his original claim through evidence from debriefing sessions (participants admitted they had believed they were giving shocks) and through film evidence where participants appeared in considerable distress when delivering the shocks.

However, the way in which Milgram's study was carried out may have been sufficient to allow some participants to recognise that they, rather than the victim, were the real subjects of the experiment. The fact that the experimenter appeared unconcerned about the learner's distress was one clue to the participants that this was not a 'real' situation. Orne and Holland cited a comparison study where 75% of the participants stated that they assumed that the victim wasn't really hurt.

Orne and Holland's second claim was that the study lacked ecological validity. They claimed that although a participant will, in an experiment, carry out behaviours that appear destructive, this reflects more on his/her willingness to trust the experimenter and the experimental context than on what she/he would do outside of the experimental situation.

Milgram's critics also argued that being ordered to give electric shocks to poor learners did not involve the same psychological processes as those that affected German prison guards in concentration camps. Milgram did not accept this criticism, arguing that although, superficially, the circumstances were less severe, the psychological processes were sufficiently similar to allow inferences to be drawn from the laboratory and applied to real life. Milgram argued that in both cases individuals stopped acting autonomously and adopted an 'agentic state', that is, acting merely as the agent of another.

question 2

Social psychology (II)

(a) Describe *two* differences between majority influence (conformity) and minority influence. (3+3 marks)

(b) Describe the procedures and findings of *one* study of minority influence. (6 marks)

(c) To what extent has research supported the view that the majority exerts a significant degree of influence over the individual? (18 marks)

Total: 30 marks

(a) This asks for more than simple definitions of majority and minority influence; it asks for *differences* between them. These might include the tendency for majority influence to produce changes in *public compliance* and minority influence to produce changes in *private acceptance*. Alternatively, you might focus on the time span of these two forms of social influence — majority influence tends to be felt almost straightaway, whereas minority influence tends to occur after a period of time. Your answer might even cover the various reasons why people yield to these different forms of social influence.

(b) Don't waste time writing about other aspects of your chosen study that are not asked for here (i.e. the aims or conclusions). The use of plurals in the question suggests that there is more than one 'procedure' and more than one 'finding'. This shouldn't worry you too much as the reporting of studies almost inevitably 'pluralises' things in this way. Although you need to include *both* procedures *and* findings to get into the top mark band, these don't have to be in the same detail or depth. Do, however, check that the study you are describing is a study of *minority* influence.

(c) As this is the AO1 + AO2 part of the question, it is not sufficient simply to *describe* research evidence that demonstrates majority influence; you are also required to *engage* with this in a critical or analytic manner. Thus, for example, you might choose to revisit some of the major studies, and look more critically at their findings to see if they really do make a good case for the power of the majority over the minority. Asch, Sherif, Crutchfield etc. are all relevant here, as is Zimbardo (people conform to the social role that they perceive is the *norm*), but use research that you feel comfortable with in this critical context.

■ ■ ■

Answer to question 2: candidate A

(a) Majority influence involves being exposed to the views of a majority, whereas minority influence involves being exposed to the views of a minority.

Majority influence tends to make people conform because they don't want to appear deviant from the rest of the group. Minority influence tends to happen despite this, therefore people are more inclined to risk the disapproval of the rest

question

of the group by going along with the minority. They might do this because the minority is more persuasive.

> There is a grain of truth in the first answer, for 1 mark, but that is all. It says nothing about these forms of influence other than that one involves exposure to the views of a minority and the other involves exposure to a majority. Remember that you are comparing two forms of social influence and so differences should reflect how or why they have their effect. The second difference provides much more information, for 2 marks, but there is some confusion over the reasons for each form of influence working, which prevents it gaining maximum marks. The answer lacks clarity which, despite the insights being presented, detracts from its overall effectiveness. (3 out of 6 marks)

(b) One of the most famous examples of minority influence was in the film *Twelve Angry Men*, in which Henry Fonda played a juror who was convinced of the innocence of a man being tried for murder. In this film, Fonda managed to win round all the other jurors (i.e. the majority) who initially were convinced of the man's guilt. In a later study, Clark used the film and showed it to students, who were then asked about the man's guilt. Some of the students simply watched the film, whereas others were told about Fonda's arguments and that others had changed their mind. Those that were told about the arguments and that others had also changed their mind were the most likely to change their own views of the man's innocence.

> This answer spends rather too much time describing the film, and perhaps not enough focusing on the actual study in which it was used. Both procedures and findings are covered, and the urge to cover other aspects of the study (i.e. aims and conclusions) has been suitably restrained. The description of procedures is a little garbled (the actual account of this study can be checked on pages 13–14), but the findings (although brief) are accurate. Under this description of the procedures, there appears to be little difference between the two conditions, so the overall answer is basic and muddled. (2 out of 6 marks)

(c) Majority influence was investigated by Asch (1953) who, in his study, found that most people were influenced at least once by the majority decision in such a way that they went against their own judgement and agreed with a wrong answer. Asch showed that the majority can be very powerful in shaping a person's opinions, although his critics claimed that this agreement was superficial, and that people who agree with a wrong answer in public do not necessarily change their real opinion in private. They go along with the majority to avoid looking stupid and experiencing the stress of disagreeing with everybody else. Although there is a difference between private acceptance and public compliance, what starts as compliance might end up as private acceptance, as people try to justify to themselves why they acted as they did in public.

Perrin and Spencer (1980) also found it difficult to produce the same findings as Asch. They found that out of over 350 trials in which the majority unanimously gave a wrong answer, only once did the participant conform to their decision.

Perrin and Spencer claimed that the only reason that Asch got the results he did was because of the time that he carried out the research. However, at the time that Perrin and Spencer were carrying out their research, other research in Belgium and the Netherlands tended to find the same results as Asch had done in the 1950s.

Although there is a lot of research supporting the influence that the majority can have on people, we must not overlook the fact that the majority influence that people experience in real life tends to be quite unlike the Asch and Perrin and Spencer studies. Real-life groups can add to this internal pressure by putting a great deal of additional pressure on deviants to make them conform.

🖉 This is a very good answer which focuses explicitly on the requirements of the question, and is not afraid to look critically at the research that has purported to demonstrate majority influence. There are some excellent insights ('…what starts as compliance might end up as private acceptance'; '…majority influence that people experience in real life tends to be quite unlike the Asch and Perrin and Spencer studies') into the complexities of this area. More could have been made of the Perrin and Spencer research — what exactly was the significance of the timing of Asch's research? The AO1 component (describing research relating to majority influence) is accurate if a little limited (4 out of 6 marks); the AO2 component is slightly limited, though effective, and is worth 10 out of 12 marks.

Total for this question: 19 out of 30 marks

▓ ▓ ▓

Answer to question 2: candidate B

🖉 The following answer is supported by material presented earlier in this book and is equivalent to a good grade-A response to this question.

(a) The type of influence that minorities can exert is different from the kind that majorities usually exert. Group members who move their opinions towards the majority are often merely complying with the majority. In contrast, the influence of minorities tends to lead members towards a private acceptance of the minority point of view.

Minority influence operates by encouraging people actively to question their own position on an issue, thereby inducing deep and long-lasting change. This often leads members to come to higher-quality decisions than if the minority viewpoint had not been present.

(b) In Moscovici et al.'s study (1969), participants were required to describe the colour of 36 slides. Of the six participants, two were confederates of the experimenter. The slides used were all blue, but the use of different filters varied their brightness. In the consistent condition of the experiment, the two confederates called all 36 slides green. In the inconsistent condition, the two confederates called 24 of the slides green and the remaining 12 slides blue.

Participants in the consistent condition yielded in 8.42% of all trials. Participants in the inconsistent condition yielded in only 1.25% of the trials. In an extension to this study, both experimental groups showed a lower threshold for green than a control group, i.e. they were more likely to report ambiguous blue/green stimuli as green.

(c) Although his research appears to suggest that conformity to the views of the majority is widespread, Asch also found that, despite the pressure exerted by the majority, a large proportion of people tend to remain independent in their judgements. Perrin and Spencer (1981) claim that the Asch studies reflect a particular historical and cultural perspective where conformity was highly valued. They suggest that such conformity effects are no longer evident in similar experimental studies.

The results of American research on conformity suggest that individuals who do not conform to the dominant norms are simply deviant and, by definition, can have no influence. Moscovici argues that the drive to reduce any disharmony from among our attitudes, beliefs and values is less important than the drive to reduce social conflict. It is social conflict and disagreement with others that create discomfort and we try to avoid that discomfort by normalising and conforming.

Moscovici's own research shows that the shift in opinion brought about by minority influence might be more enduring than that brought about by majority influence. Although a majority can bring about compliance, it doesn't necessarily believe in it. A minority, on the other hand, can bring about internalisation — the individuals affected actually 'believe in' the minority's values.

Asch's experiment has been criticised for being unrealistic to the extent that in the real world we expect to take decisions on subjects more complex and more important than the length of a line. However, his research reveals that group pressure can be so strong that we are willing to deny the evidence of our own eyes for the sake of conformity with the rest of the group.

Social psychology (III)

(a) Outline *two* explanations of why people yield to majority influence. (3+3 marks)

(b) Outline the aims and conclusions of *one* research study of obedience to authority. (6 marks)

(c) With reference to *one or more* research studies of social influence, consider whether such research might be considered unethical. (18 marks)

Total: 30 marks

(a) Although there are many reasons *why* people yield to majority influence, the most commonly quoted are **normative social influence** (people conform so as not to appear different, and out of a desire to be liked) and **informational social influence** (people conform because they believe others may have more information than they do themselves). Remember that each of these is marked independently, so spend equal amounts of time on both.

(b) As with all questions that ask for specific aspects of a study, this should be approached carefully. The study does *not* ask for the procedures or the findings, so don't waste time putting these in as well. Outlining the aims requires a statement of what the researcher(s) was trying to find out, i.e. their rationale for carrying out the study, while an outline of the 'conclusions' requires more than a simple statement of the main findings. For example, Milgram found that 65% of his participants gave the full 450 volts, and all went up to the 300-volt level (these are *findings*). A conclusion, on the other hand, might be that obedience to malevolent authority appears to be a consequence of the situation a person finds him/herself in (e.g. in a high status institution, with a powerful authority figure) rather than some underlying pathological condition of the individual.

(c) Although there is no requirement to focus on one specific form of social influence, it is most likely that you will choose Milgram's research on obedience to authority. This research raised many critical points concerning its ethical issues. Don't just *describe* these criticisms, but try to develop a *commentary* on them. For example, you might consider the costs and benefits of such research, and whether the ethical criticisms from people such as Baumrind were justified. Remember that this is the AO2 component of the question, requiring you to *engage* with the topic in an evaluative and analytic way.

■ ■ ■

Answer to question 3: candidate A

(a) People yield to majority influence because if they didn't the majority could make it very unpleasant for them. If people go along with the majority, however, they might believe that they are more likely to be accepted by the others in the group. Going against the majority can be very difficult because of the stress of acting or thinking differently.

Another explanation for why people yield to majority influence is because there are strong adaptive reasons for doing so. Because groups need to stay together to help each other, doing the same as everyone else might be a good way of ensuring that the group stays close and that outsiders are excluded. Groups that are tightly knit may have a better chance of surviving than groups that are not, so this characteristic evolves within the gene line.

> There isn't a lot else one could say when describing normative social influence. It doesn't matter that the term 'normative influence' hasn't been used in the first answer, because most of the important points are included, for full marks. An impressive and very different explanation, accurate and well argued, is provided in the second answer. The way in which this 'groupishness' is passed along the gene line is not that clear, but this is an exam on social psychology, not genetics, so the answer is worth full marks. (6 out of 6 marks)

(b) Milgram was interested in finding out the conditions under which people would obey an authority figure. He advertised for participants to take part in a study on the relationship between punishment and learning. The participants drew lots to see who would be the learner and who would be the teacher, though the 'real' participant always played the part of the teacher, giving gradually increasing electric shocks to the learner whenever the latter gave a wrong answer. Milgram's conclusions were that nearly two thirds of his participants gave the maximum shock, even when the 'learner' appeared to be dead already (no real shocks were given, as the 'learner' was really an actor). Those participants who tried to leave the experiment were told by the experimenter that they had to stay, and nobody left before giving 300 volts.

> This is an unfortunate waste of time — the answer briefly outlines one of the aims of Milgram's study of obedience, but then gives details of the *procedures* and *findings* of this study (*not* required) and makes no attempt to outline the *conclusions* (which are required). This is a cautionary tale: make sure you answer the question set and don't simply regurgitate all you can remember about a study despite its lack of relevance to the question. (1 out of 6 marks)

(c) Milgram and Zimbardo carried out research into different aspects of social influence. Both of these might be considered unethical. Milgram's obedience research was shocking because he deceived his participants and he did not get their informed consent to take part in the study. He used experimental 'prods' to make them continue when they wanted to give up. This meant he was coercing them to take part in the research rather than letting them continue because they wanted to. He had no right to harm them in the way that he did, and his participants might have experienced long-term distress because they had been a part of the study.

Zimbardo carried out a prison simulation study in which he locked people up and let them act out the role of either prisoner or guard. The guards were brutal in their treatment of the prisoners and the experiment had to be stopped earlier than planned. As with Milgram's research, Zimbardo harmed his participants and did not have their consent to lock them up. There was also a good deal of deception going on as participants thought they really had been arrested and sent to jail. The study was only halted when Zimbardo's fiancée made him stop because she thought it was wrong to carry on and cause such pain.

e There are two appropriate research studies used in this answer. The answer details some of the claims concerning the unethical nature of Milgram's study, although it does not consider either Milgram's response to these accusations or the wider issues that they raise. Although such 'two-sided' debate is not obligatory for these questions, it is a good way of developing a critical commentary and thus fulfilling the AO2 requirements in your response. In among the accurate detail concerning both of these studies, there is a fair amount of speculation ('participants might have experienced long-term distress') and inaccuracy ('did not have their consent to lock them up'). Overall, the answer is reasonable but limited in its coverage of the topic. The AO1 content receives 3 out of 6 marks (generally accurate but limited) and the AO2 content, being basic and not particularly effective, receives 5 out of 12 marks.

Total for this question: 15 out of 30 marks

■ ■ ■

Answer to question 3: candidate B

e The following answer is suported by material presented earlier in this book and is equivalent to a good grade-A response to this question.

(a) The subject is able to shift the responsibility for their actions onto another person (in this case the experimenter) through the process of agentic shift. They now see themselves as the agents of another person (the authority figure) and no longer responsible for their own actions.

In Milgram's original study, the teacher and learner were in different rooms, with the teacher protected (i.e. buffered) from having to see their 'victim', and also from the consequences of the electric shocks. When the learner was in the same room, this buffer effect was reduced, as was the tendency to obey the commands of the experimenter, and therefore the overall level of obedience.

(b) One of the main aims of Milgram's research into obedience to authority was to explore the circumstances under which people might be induced to act against their conscience by inflicting harm on other people. This was born out of the need to explain the behaviour of those who committed atrocities in the Second World War death camps.

Prior to Milgram's research, it was traditional for social scientists to explain behaviour such as the Nazi war crimes in terms of deviant personalities. Milgram showed that destructive obedience can be evoked in the majority of people by purely situational factors. The capacity for moral decision-making is suspended when an individual is embedded within a powerful social hierarchy.

question

(c) On publication, Milgram's findings generated a wide range of commentary. Some decided that Milgram had accomplished some of the most morally significant investigations in modern psychology (Elms, 1972). Others described Milgram's work as 'a momentous and meaningful contribution to our knowledge of human behaviour' (Erikson, 1968). In sharp contrast, one critic decided that Milgram himself had behaved immorally, deceiving his participants and persuading them to perform this distasteful task. No matter what they revealed, his findings were not worth the tension and self-doubt they created in his participants (Baumrind, 1964).

The basic ethical question in this research seems to be whether any possible discomfort incurred by participants collectively outweighed possible insights into atrocities in the real world, such as the behaviour of the Nazis in the Second World War. Many of Milgram's participants experienced tension, doubt and self-recrimination; they exhibited clear signs of discomfort, and most decided that they had to resist authority more effectively in the future. Thus, the question still stands: on balance, was this research justifiable? This ethical question involves value judgements about the feelings of research participants and about the role of research in society.

Milgram employed procedures to protect the participants. For example, all participants were informed of the basic experimental procedures at the outset. His debriefing sessions included a meeting between the teacher and the unharmed learner, as well as extended discussion with the authority figure. Some weeks later, all participants received a five-page report, including a questionnaire asking them to express once again their thoughts and feelings about the experience. Most recommended more experiments of this nature, and replied that they had learned something important to them personally. For Milgram, this finding constituted the central justification of this research: the participants judged it as acceptable and worthwhile.

Social psychology (IV)

(a) What is meant by the terms 'social influence', 'conformity' and 'ethical issue'? (2+2+2 marks)

(b) With reference to the study of social influence, describe two ethical issues that have arisen in such research. (3+3 marks)

(c) To what extent have psychologists been successful in dealing with the ethical issues that arise in psychological research? (18 marks)

Total: 30 marks

(a) These three terms can be defined using the definitions on pages 21–22. You are not required to offer such elaborate definitions, but the more accurate and detailed your definitions, the more likely it is that you will pick up full marks. Be careful not to confuse an ethical *issue* with an ethical *guideline*.

(b) There are two main ways to go wrong in this question. First, you might ignore the 'with reference to the study of social influence' part of the question. Second, you might describe ethical *guidelines* rather than ethical *issues* (there is an important distinction between these). You should describe two ethical issues that you feel were a feature of one or more studies of social influence (for example, the research of Milgram or Zimbardo), and then demonstrate how they were a feature of your chosen studies. Remember, this is a 3+3 mark question, so balance your answer accordingly.

(c) Before responding to this part of the question, it would pay to read it again *very carefully*. The question does not ask you simply to describe how psychologists have dealt with the ethical issues that arise in psychological research (although this might form the AO1 component of the answer) but asks whether such attempts have been successful (this is the AO2 component). As with all such questions, the AO2 component is worth more (12 marks) than the AO1 component (6 marks), so this fact should guide your response to this question. Although there are a number of ways in which this question could be answered, a critical appraisal of the role and effectiveness of ethical guidelines is probably the most obvious way. Don't get drawn into simply listing the BPS ethical guidelines — that clearly is *not* answering the question. As with all AO1 + AO2 questions, this one calls for you to *engage* with the material in a critical manner.

■ ■ ■

Answer to question 4: candidate A

(a) Social influence is where other people have an effect on us, such as in conformity and obedience.

Conformity is where we go along with other people because we want to be like them.

An ethical issue is an instruction on how to behave in psychological research. For example, not deceiving people is an ethical issue.

🖉 The first is a fairly basic definition, as it tells us nothing about the kind of 'effect' that other people have on us. However, for 1 mark it does give us the insight that this is a form of influence involving other people, and illustrates this with appropriate examples. As with the first, the second is basic and lacking in detail and loses 1 mark. Conformity does involve us 'going along with other people', and one explanation of conformity is that we do this because we want to be like them and accepted by them. An ethical issue is *not* an instruction about how to behave in psychological research (that is an ethical *guideline*), but not deceiving people is an example of an ethical issue, for 1 mark. (3 out of 6 marks)

(b) One ethical issue is deception. Deception means misleading participants in research or withholding some important details of the research. Deception is wrong because, like in Milgram's obedience research, people cannot give their informed consent since they do not have all the information they need.

A second ethical issue is protection from harm. In Milgram's research, participants were exposed to high levels of personal stress. It might also be argued that, although no real shocks were given, Milgram had no right to 'reveal' to participants the fact that they were capable of such behaviour. Researchers have a responsibility to safeguard the well-being of their research participants, and critics of Milgram's research suggest that he failed in this respect.

🖉 The first answer provides a description of *deception* as an ethical issue. This is quite a competent answer except that, other than a throw-away mention of Milgram, there is no reference to social influence research. This might just get a generous 2 out of 3 marks. The second is a much more competent answer, for full marks, and one that addresses all aspects of the question. It describes an appropriate ethical issue and contextualises this accurately within Milgram's obedience research. (5 out of 6 marks)

(c) Ethical guidelines, such as those used by the BPS and APA, are specifically developed to help protect the interests of people who take part in research. These guidelines stop researchers having to take difficult decisions when they are faced with an ethical dilemma, which is a choice between two courses of action, such as deception or telling the truth. An example of a guideline is that researchers should not deceive participants and must obtain full informed consent before using a participant in the research.

One thing that ethical guidelines don't deal with is the type of research that researchers can carry out, or even what they might do with the results of the research. Some research, for example studies into race differences in IQ or genetic influences on homosexuality, is potentially harmful, yet ethical guidelines offer little or no advice about the potential consequences of carrying out such research.

A second way in which psychologists have been successful in dealing with ethical issues is through the ethical review committees in universities. These committees scrutinise all potential research in the planning stage, and permission must be given before the research can continue. However, some important research cannot be carried out if it offends the committee or if it might produce an adverse public reaction. Because of this, although an ethical review committee might serve an important monitoring role, it can also serve to inhibit progress in important areas of research.

The first paragraph of this answer provides a good account of the nature of ethical guidelines. This is coupled with the fact that there are more good descriptive points elsewhere in the answer (6 out of 6 marks for AO1). The second paragraph offers the contention that although ethical guidelines are effective in the localised 'management' of psychological research, they tend not to address some of the wider ethical issues in psychological research. There is commendable awareness of the censorial role of ethical review committees which tempers their more important (perhaps) monitoring role in the planning stages of psychological research. This answer allows itself, on occasion, to drift back to the AO1 requirements of the question (i.e. it tends towards description rather than evaluation and analysis), but it is a reasonable, if slightly limited, critical account of this area. More could have been made of the AO2 material in this answer. (6 out of 12 marks for AO2)

Total for this question: 20 out of 30 marks

Answer to question 4: candidate B

The following answer is supported by material presented earlier in this book and is equivalent to a good grade-A response to this question.

(a) Social influence refers to the various processes (such as majority and minority influence) by which a person's attitudes, beliefs and behaviours are modified by the presence or actions of others.

Conformity is a form of social influence that results from exposure to the opinions of a majority. It is the tendency for people to adopt the behaviour, attitudes and values of other members of a reference group.

An ethical issue arises in research where there are conflicting sets of values concerning the goals, procedures or outcomes of a research study. For example, researchers must weigh up the importance of gaining full informed consent from participants, against the scientific importance of observing behaviour as it occurs naturally in different social settings.

(b) Deception involves the withholding of information or the misleading of research participants. Baumrind claimed that Milgram, in his study of obedience, had deceived his participants on two counts. First, he had led them to believe they were taking part in a study on the effects of punishment on learning. Second, he had then led them to believe they were actually delivering electric shocks.

The principle of informed consent is that research participants should be allowed to agree or refuse to participate, in the light of comprehensive information concerning the nature and purpose of the research. Although Milgram's participants had given their permission to take part in a study on the relationship between punishment and learning, they had not given their consent to take part in a study of obedience to authority. Therefore, they had not given their informed consent to take part in this study.

(c) Although psychologists deal with ethical issues in their research in many ways (e.g. through professional training), the use of ethical guidelines or 'codes of conduct' remains the most effective way of dealing appropriately with such issues. The 'role' of ethical guidelines is summarised in the *BPS Code of Conduct* (1993): 'to preserve an overriding high regard for the well-being and dignity of research participants'.

Ethical guidelines tend to be based on a 'cost–benefit' approach, in that scientific ends are sometimes seen as justifying the use of methods that sometimes sacrifice participants' welfare, particularly when the research promises 'the greatest good for the greatest number'. This is not always foolproof, as costs and benefits are impossible to predict accurately prior to conducting a study, and there are often different recipients of the costs and benefits of an investigation. Baumrind (1975) objects to cost–benefit ways of resolving ethical conflicts. Such analyses inevitably lead to moral dilemmas (i.e. establishing the relative importance of costs and benefits), yet the function of ethical guidelines is precisely to avoid such dilemmas.

Most professional codes, particularly those in the social sciences, have very little power of censure. Although the BPS Chartered Psychologist status does go some way to controlling the activities of members of the profession, exclusion from a professional body does not prevent social scientists from continuing to carry out research. Ethical guidelines might protect the immediate needs of research participants, but might not deal with all the possible ways in which research can inflict harm on a group of people or section of society (e.g. members of a particular racial, gender or sexual group). The Canadian Psychological Association, however, advises its members to 'analyse likely short-term, ongoing, and long-term risks and benefits of each course of action on the individual(s)/group(s) involved or likely to be affected'.

Research methods (I)

A psychologist wanted to investigate whether travelling sales representatives' gender and their tendency to answer a mobile phone call while driving are associated. A random sample of 50 male and 50 female travelling sales representatives was recruited. These participants were asked to recall one occasion when they had answered a mobile phone call received while driving and could have chosen whether or not to stop their car to answer it. They were asked to state whether they had or had not stopped to answer the phone. Results were summarised graphically, as shown in Figure 1. The external validity of these findings was checked by making a mobile phone call to the participants when they were known to be driving (a naturalistic setting) and recording whether they did or did not stop their car to answer the call.

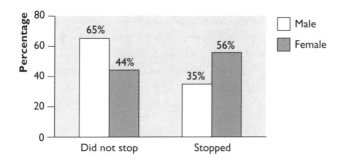

Figure 1 Percentages of male and female sales representatives who reported stopping their cars to answer a mobile phone call

(a) Suggest a suitable null hypothesis for this investigation. (2 marks)

(b) How might the psychologist have selected their random sample? (2 marks)

(c) Outline *one* advantage of using a random sample. (2 marks)

(d) Explain *one* other way in which the psychologist might have sampled participants for this study. (2 marks)

(e) Outline *one* advantage and *one* disadvantage of the questionnaire as a way of carrying out psychological research. (2 + 2 marks)

(f) Give *two* conclusions that might be drawn from Figure 1. (2 + 2 marks)

(g) What is meant by *external validity*? (2 marks)

(h) Explain why it was thought necessary to check the external validity of the findings of this study. (3 marks)

(i) Identify *one* ethical problem raised by the way in which the external validity of this study was checked, and outline *one* way in which this might have been dealt with. (3 marks)

(j) The psychologist believes from her observations that people who answer the telephone while driving are less attentive to other things happening around them and so are more likely to make mistakes. Outline the procedures of a possible laboratory experiment that could be carried out to test this belief. (6 marks)

Total: 30 marks

e This study comprises a brief questionnaire survey, the findings of which are checked using naturalistic observation. Responses have been categorised according to whether a driver is male or female and whether they did or did not stop to answer a mobile phone call while driving. Care has been taken in the design to ensure that drivers recalled a real-life occasion when they clearly did have the chance to stop to answer the phone call. As with any survey, good sampling is important and parts (b) and (d) address this. A further issue is the extent to which you can trust what participants say in surveys. Checking the validity of their responses in another setting (parts (g) and (h)) is important, but is not without its problems (part (i)). Part (j) requires a (brief) outline of how this study might be extended to test a specific aspect of the relationship between mobile phone use and driver behaviour. Testing this in a laboratory requires some degree of *simulation*, such as participants having to respond to an extraneous stimulus whilst also completing some other task (such as a driving simulation). Only the procedures are required (not the aims, hypotheses or any potential findings) and marks would be awarded for the degree of accuracy (i.e. whether such procedures would be appropriate in this context) and detail in the response. There is no one right answer to this question, and you would be marked on your inventiveness rather than your ability to remember the details of real studies in this area.

■ ■ ■

Answer to question 5: candidate A

(a) There will be no difference between the different sexes in their mobile phone use.

> *e* Look at the text in the question to help you give a more accurate answer. In this case, a little rewording is all that is necessary, for example: 'There is no association between a travelling sales representative's sex and their tendency to answer a mobile phone call while driving'. (1 out of 2 marks)

(b) They could put all the names in a hat and pull out the number they need.

> *e* This answer is too brief for the full 2 marks. It should make some reference to the population being sampled (e.g. sales representatives within a large sales force) and the actual sample (50 males and 50 females) that are selected by this method. (1 out of 2 marks)

(c) An advantage of using a random sample is that it is random, not biased.

> *e* This is another answer that is too brief and more than a little circular ('a random sample…is random'). This is partly accurate, although the most important aspect of a random sample (that every member of the population has an equal chance of being selected) is missing. (1 out of 2 marks).

(d) An opportunity sample would involve using a group of participants who were available at the time (e.g. a group of sales representatives who were attending a conference).

🖉 Good use of a feasible example here helps to secure 2 out of 2 marks.

(e) One advantage is that it is cheap. One disadvantage is that people can say what they think you want to hear. They try to look good and may not tell the truth.

🖉 The advantage given here, although quite common in response to this question, gets no marks. Cheap relative to what? The use of questionnaires may be extremely expensive if many have to be distributed, mailed back, analysed etc. Claims such as this must be subtantiated. If the student had justified this claim (e.g. by arguing that the quantitative data produced might be cheaper to analyse in terms of person hours than the more complex qualitative data produced in less structured interviews) then the answer would be accepted. The disadvantage is better and has sufficient detail (social desirability bias) for the full 2 marks.

(f) Males engage in more risky behaviour than females. Not many people stop their cars to answer their mobile phones.

🖉 The first part is a rather general answer, for 1 mark, although not without merit. The use of the word 'risky' is over-stating what the data really are telling us. An accurate and informed answer would say that more males than females did not stop to answer a mobile phone call while driving and more females than males did stop. The second conclusion given is also too general (1 mark). It would have been better to say that 'more people did not stop their cars when taking a mobile phone call than did stop, and this was evident for both males and females. (2 out of 4 marks)

(g) External validity means that the results can be generalised to other situations or to other groups of people.

🖉 This explanation is accurate and informed. It identifies both population and ecological validity, which is commendable, although just one, properly explained, would have been enough. (2 out of 2 marks)

(h) The results had to be checked to see if the participants acted the same way while actually driving.

🖉 This explanation is too brief. It needs to go on to say why checking the findings matters. For example, it is useful to know whether the initial findings are specific to the testing situation. (1 out of 3 marks)

(i) It could be argued that the investigator was not protecting the well-being of drivers — tempting them to answer the phone while driving put them at risk. They should have found another way to check the external validity that didn't put them at risk.

🖉 The ethical issue identified (protection of participants from harm) is appropriate and accurate, so 1 mark for that. Although there is some understanding of what would be an appropriate way of overcoming this problem, there is insufficient detail for any of the other 2 marks available. It would have been better to suggest an alternative, or suggest how the likelihood of harm might have been averted (e.g. only using private roads where there would be no other traffic). (1 out of 3 marks)

question

(j) The psychologist could set up an experiment where participants have to play on a driving game (such as Carmaggedon). She could have two conditions. One condition would be to play the game without interruptions and the other would be to play it, but every so often there would be something else they would have to do that took their attention away from the game for a moment. The psychologist could then see if there was a difference in performance between the two conditions.

The experiment suggested here is appropriate (two conditions, separated by the presence of the independent variable) and the use of a simulation and distraction task is mentioned. The outcome (difference between conditions) is also quantified. A better answer might have mentioned the sampling, experimental design, nature of the distraction task, any important extraneous variables and how the dependent variable would have been measured. However, this is generally accurate, if less detailed, and is worth 4 out of 6 marks.

Total for this question: 17 out of 30 marks

■ ■ ■

Answer to question 5: candidate B

The following answer is supported by material presented earlier in this book and is equivalent to a good grade-A response to this question; in this case, full marks would be awarded.

(a) There is no association between the gender of a travelling sales representative and his/her tendency to answer a mobile phone call while driving.

(b) The psychologist should draw up full lists of all the male and female sales reps within a particular population (such as a large sales force) and, using random number tables, select 50 males from the male list and 50 females from the female list.

(c) An advantage of the random sample is that each member of the population has an equal chance of being selected. Therefore, there is less chance of the sample being biased.

(d) A quota sampling technique could be used. The researcher could attend an event that sales representatives would attend, determine the proportions of males and females in the conference population and obtain participants for the sample in the same proportions.

(e) An advantage of the questionnaire is that it allows the researcher flexibility to ask open questions (producing more detailed responses) or closed questions (which can produce a great amount of information relevant to the research).

A disadvantage of the questionnaire is that there may be only a small proportion of questionnaires returned and so it is difficult for the researcher to be confident that those who do return their questionnaires are representative of those who do not.

(f) Generally, more people do not stop their car to answer a mobile phone call compared with those who do stop their car. More females than males stop their car to answer a mobile phone call.

(g) External validity refers to whether research findings can also be observed outside the original research situation, when applied either to different groups of people (population validity) or to different situations (ecological validity).

(h) An obvious problem with questioning people about potentially unacceptable behaviour is that they might give selective or dishonest responses. Testing the validity of the findings in another setting can help the researcher to check whether this is happening.

(i) Deception is involved in this part of the study. Participants would be unable to give informed consent before taking part in the study and this is an intrusion on their freedom. The psychologist could explain to a representative sample of sales representatives about the deception and ask if they would have consented to have taken part in those circumstances. If they said yes, then it could be assumed that the real participants would also have agreed in those circumstances.

(j) The psychologist might use a matched participants design, matching participants in terms of their driving experience, eyesight and any other important variables that might influence their performance on a driving simulator. In one condition, participants would have to navigate their 'car' along a track with many obstacles and changes in driving conditions. During each 1-hour simulation, they would be required to answer a mobile telephone and engage in meaningful conversation with the experimenter for a 1-minute period. This would be repeated ten times over the hour. The second condition would involve the same simulation, but without the telephone interruptions. The computer would record the number of errors they make (e.g. obstacles hit or road instructions missed) in the two conditions.

Research methods (II)

A team of psychologists is interested in the possible relationship between level of belief in telepathy (the ability to transmit and receive thoughts from one person to another) and success in a telepathy test. After first carrying out a pilot study, they advertise in a Sunday newspaper for people willing to be tested as part of this study. Over the following weeks, they test 1000 people in a university laboratory. The participants are asked to indicate their level of belief in telepathy. They are then asked to choose one from four alternative shapes as the experimenter attempts to 'transmit' the correct shape to them. This is repeated 100 times and the percentage of shapes identified correctly is calculated. The psychologists then correlate the level of belief and the number of shapes (out of 100) identified correctly. This produces a correlation coefficient of +0.7.

(a) State a suitable directional hypothesis for this study. (2 marks)

(b) Explain how level of belief in telepathy might be operationalised. (2 marks)

(c) Explain how the psychologists' expectations about the outcome of the study might have affected the results obtained, and outline how this might have been overcome. (2 + 2 marks)

(d) Explain how the results of this study might have been influenced by demand characteristics. (3 marks)

(e) Explain the benefit of using a pilot study before a study. (2 marks)

(f) Explain *one* advantage and *one* disadvantage of using a correlational analysis in this study. (2 + 2 marks)

(g) Explain how the method of obtaining participants might have affected the validity of any findings. (3 marks)

(h) Outline *one* way that the psychologists might have ensured that there was no cheating during the telepathy test. (2 marks)

(i) Explain *one* ethical issue that might apply to this study and outline how the psychologists might have dealt with it. (2 + 2 marks)

(j) Which correlation coefficient represents a stronger relationship between two variables, +0.4 or –0.6? (1 mark)

(k) Describe *one* way in which the psychologists might have checked the reliability of their findings. (3 marks)

Total: 30 marks

e This study involves collecting data that can be subjected to correlational analysis. Each participant provides a score indicating their level of belief in telepathy and another which is their telepathy score. These data can be presented visually in a scattergraph and numerically in a correlation coefficient. This question invites you to show your understanding of these concepts in (d) and (e). You must also formulate a suitably worded hypothesis in (a), and show that you understand the need for precision — (b) — and control — (c). Part (f) simply asks you how the reliability of the findings could be checked. You do not have to explain why.

Answer to question 6: candidate A

(a) There is a relationship between level of belief in telepathy and success in a telepathy test.

> 🖉 There is no direction (positive or negative) specified in this answer, so it is incorrect. (0 out of 2 marks)

(b) Belief in telepathy could be operationalised by asking people to rate their belief on a scale of 1 (no belief) to 10 (total belief).

> 🖉 This is an appropriate method of operationalising belief in telepathy, and is suitably detailed. (2 out of 2 marks)

(c) The psychologists might have been trying extra hard with the people who said they believed in telepathy, but not as hard with those who said they didn't believe in telepathy. They could overcome this by using different experimenters for each condition.

> 🖉 This is an accurate and detailed explanation of an experimenter effect (so 2 out of 2 marks), but the method of overcoming it is hopelessly confused. This candidate seems under the impression that this is an experiment rather than a correlational analysis and it is by no means clear how using different experimenters would overcome this particular experimenter effect (0 out of 2 marks).

(d) Participants might have tried to impress the experimenter by trying hard.

> 🖉 There is some degree of appropriate detail here, but it is basic and doesn't really address the question explicitly. It would have been better to explain that 'trying hard' might have meant trying to match their performance on the telepathy test with their previously stated level of belief in telepathy. 'Impressing the experimenter' might have been expanded to mention that the participants were looking for cues in the experimenter's behaviour or manner that would guide the way they were to respond (e.g. when stating their level of belief in telepathy). (1 out of 3 marks)

(e) One benefit is that it lets the researcher try everything out before the study itself.

> 🖉 This answer requires more detail. The candidate should, perhaps, have explained what 'trying everything out' actually means, and what the researchers might then do as a result of any feedback from the pilot study. (1 out of 2 marks).

(f) Correlational analysis helps us to show whether two things are related in some way.
> Although they may be related, it doesn't mean that one thing (e.g. belief in telepathy) has caused the other (performance on a test of telepathy).

> 🖉 The first answer is correct, but too brief, and so loses 1 mark. This is an occasion when an example would convince the examiner that the candidate understands what 'related' means. The second answer gains full marks. Although the investigators might not have been looking for a causal relationship between these two

variables, the inability of a correlational analysis to provide one is an acceptable and appropriate disadvantage in this context. (3 out of 4 marks)

(g) The participants were a random sample of people who read this particular newspaper, so it might not have been representative.

   The candidate has mistakenly identified this as a random sample (it isn't — it is a volunteer sample), but this can be ignored as the question doesn't ask for an identification of the sampling method. The use of a possibly unrepresentative sample (from the readers of just one newspaper) is appropriate, although it might have been expanded a little to add more detail. (2 out of 3 marks)

(h) The person sending the message might have been doing something that gave the receiver a hint about the shape they were sending (e.g. doing something with the tone of their voice).

   Although the problem is clearly identified, there is no attempt to offer a suggestion for how it might be overcome (which is the requirement of the question). Unfortunately, this receives no marks.

(i) One issue is that participants may feel bad about themselves if they don't do well. The psychologists could debrief them afterwards.

   Some questions (such as this one) offer a clear indication that expansion is necessary for the full marks available. This candidate has *identified* an appropriate issue rather than explaining it fully (so 1 out of 2 marks), and offered only the briefest statement of how the psychologists might deal with it (1 out of 2 marks).

(j) +0.4 is stronger

   A sneaky question perhaps, but this shows that this particular candidate cannot *interpret* correlation coefficients. When determining the *strength* of a correlation, the sign (+ or −) is irrelevant. (0 marks)

(k) One way would be to take lots of measurements of telepathy. That way, it would be less likely that the results could be down to chance.

   The second sentence just rescues the second mark, although a secure, accurate and informed response would mention the need to compare the different measurements to see if they were consistent. (2 out of 3 marks)

Total for this question: 15 out of 30 marks

■ ■ ■

Answer to question 6: candidate B

   The following answer is supported by material presented earlier in this book and is equivalent to a good grade-A response to this question; in this case, full marks would be awarded.

(a) There is a positive relationship between level of belief in telepathy and success in a telepathy task.

(b) Participants could be given a questionnaire to test their level of belief. Scores from this would indicate the extent to which they believed in telepathy.

(c) If the psychologists believe that there is a relationship between level of belief in telepathy and telepathic ability, this might unconsciously influence the way they act with participants with different levels of belief, and so affect the results. They could deal with this by using a double-blind procedure — not letting the 'sender' know the hypothesis or the participant's level of belief.

(d) The participants may be able to pick up cues from the experimenter about how they are to behave. For example, if they guess the nature of the hypothesis, then those with low levels of belief in telepathy may not try particularly hard to get the shapes right.

(e) A pilot study enables the researcher to identify any problems with the research design during a 'dry run' of the investigation. These problems can then be corrected in advance of the main study.

(f) Correlational analysis enables us to determine whether there is a linear relationship between the two variables of interest and, if so, its direction and strength.
Correlation is a description of relationships between variables. It does not allow us to say one variable causes changes in another — something an experiment might allow us to do.

(g) Because the psychologists have used a volunteer sample from a Sunday newspaper, this may prove to be unrepresentative on two counts. First, those who volunteer may believe they actually do have telepathic powers. Second, the sample is restricted to the readers of just one newspaper, and might not be generalisable beyond this group of people.

(h) They might have placed the experimenter and the participant out of eye and voice contact with each other so that there could be no facial or vocal cues that might help the participant to guess correctly the shape being transmitted.

(i) One possible ethical issue is 'protection of participants from psychological harm', in that some participants may experience a loss of self-esteem if they perform poorly on the test of telepathy. This can be overcome by not making scores available, or by making them available only to each participant individually and offering appropriate debriefing that returns the participant to the same psychological state he/she was in at the beginning of the investigation.

(j) −0.6

(k) It would be necessary to re-test the participants on another occasion. Scores from the second testing occasion could then be compared with the scores from the first occasion, to see whether they were consistent.